TRUST ME

THE TRUE STORY OF CONFESSION KILLER HENRY LEE LUCAS

RYAN GREEN

For Helen, Harvey, Frankie and Dougie

Disclaimer

This book is about real people committing real crimes. The story has been constructed by facts but some of the scenes, dialogue and characters have been fictionalised.

Polite Note to the Reader

This book is written in British English except where fidelity to other languages or accents are appropriate. Some words and phrases may differ from US English.

Copyright © Ryan Green 2019

All rights reserved

ISBN: 9781091583870

YOUR FREE BOOK IS WAITING

From bestselling author Ryan Green

There is a man who is officially classed as "**Britain's most dangerous prisoner**"

The man's name is Robert Maudsley, and his crimes earned him the nickname "**Hannibal the Cannibal**"

This free book is an exploration of his story...

amazonkindle   **nook**   **kobo**   **iBooks**

★★★★★ *"Ryan brings the horrifying details to life. I can't wait to read more by this author!"*

Get a free copy of **Robert Maudsley: Hannibal the Cannibal** when you sign up to join my Reader's Group.

www.ryangreenbooks.com/free-book

CONTENTS

Hear My Confession 7

The Son of a Whore 15

Growing Pains 26

The Dying Light 34

A Boy Named Sue 44

Making the Perfect Killer 52

A Match Made in Hell 64

The Grand Tour 69

The Child Bride 76

Abandonment Issues 83

Alone at Last 93

The Downward Spiral 102

Anything You Say 109

Fruit of the Poisoned Tree 117

The Perfect Liars 125

Want More? 128

Every Review Helps 129

About Ryan Green 130

More Books by Ryan Green 131

Free True Crime Audiobook 135

Hear My Confession

The car lay unmoving by the side of the highway; not with the cold stillness of a dead thing, but the waiting stillness of a coiled rattlesnake, just waiting for its time to strike. Out here in the middle of nowhere the desolation of the American South was abundantly present. There were deserts and icebergs with more life spread across them than this little slice of nothing. Nothing to see, and nothing to do, except each other.

There was no urgency to the sex—the car wasn't even rocking on its suspension. There was no love and not even much desire if truth be told. Ottis's face was pressed into the fabric of the backseat, his snaggletooth snagging on the tattered stitching when he turned his head for air. They were both slick with sweat, their clothes plastered onto the hard planes of their bodies. The windows were fogged up and the air was muggy with the air conditioning turned off. Henry loomed over Ottis's back, his mouth hanging open in a perpetual silent moan. In the dim light of the car, with his brows drawn down and furrowed, it looked like he had no eyes at all—two dark caves instead of the one empty socket that was usually on display. There was no love, no urgency, no desire, just the mechanical rocking motion that helped them to pass the time until the phone rang.

That was the one feature of this stretch of nowhere that nobody had mentioned before: the payphone standing proud out of the sand at the roadside, just waiting to be used when some poor unfortunate broke down out here with no help in a hundred miles. You wouldn't think that a phone like that would even have a number to receive calls, but you'd be wrong. It was the reason that Henry and Ottis were waiting here. The sharp song of that phone ringing was what they both strained to hear over the sound of their own harsh breathing and grunting. It was due any moment now.

The sun dipped low towards the horizon, cherry red and wavering behind the rising heat of the day. Sunset was the appointed time for their call, but the fall of darkness here and the fall of darkness down in Florida could be at different times. Neither Henry nor Ottis had the education required to decipher it themselves, so they waited patiently by the phone, doing what came naturally while the hours rolled on by.

There was no end to this for either one of them. In the heat and the dark, they were too exhausted to exert the efforts required to push over the edge into a moment of real pleasure, but their lusts would not settle until they'd been sated, so they rocked on and on.

The phone began to ring.

Henry slipped out of Ottis and out of the side door of the car before the other man had the time to even groan in protest. By all rights, Ottis should be the one answering the call. He was the one who had been chosen. He was the one who had been marked by his grandmother and the devil. Henry made him weak, made him hand over control of the things that should have been his, and his alone. That was just how powerful Henry was, how majestic.

Henry picked up the phone with his jeans still halfway up his legs. Wasn't like there was anybody out here to see him anyway.

'Tell me, child, do you accept Satan as your lord and master?'

Henry chuckled into the mouthpiece. All confident swagger even in the face of a question like that. 'You know that I do.'

The voice on the phone was guttural and monstrous, enough to turn the hair of lesser men white. 'And will you serve the dark majesty with all of the strength in your body?'

'Most definitely.' Henry was still smirking like this was all a game to him. Ottis had tumbled out onto the tarmac, knees near searing at the touch of it. He flinched every time Henry was coy with their masters. Every little joke or jibe that he made filled Ottis with terror.

'Are you ready to fulfil your purpose in the grand design of our Lord and master, Satan, the Dark Angel!?'

Henry gave Ottis a wink. 'Just tell me where to go and what to do.'

'There is a town, four hundred miles to the west of where you now stand, and outside of that town, you shall find a girl. Her hair is long and dark. Her skin is pale and freckled. She will be carrying a backpack with a purple lotus flower embroidered upon it. You shall know her by these signs, and you shall take her. Kill the girl and bring our master's plan of chaos closer to fruition. Do what you will with the body afterwards. Take whatever pleasure in it that Satan will allow you. But first, be sure to send her soul down into the pits of hell for him to feast upon.'

'As you command.' The words came clumsily to Henry's cocky mouth. He didn't take kindly to orders, even when they came from the Prince of Darkness himself. 'You are our hands, and through you, we shall work His infernal will. You are the Hands of Death, and with each killing, we shall spread more terror and dissension across this great nation until it falls to its knees.' The next words seemed to be drawn out of Henry involuntarily, like a howl. He threw back his head and bellowed, 'Hail Satan!'

'Hail Satan!' echoed both the phone and Ottis, Ottis from his place in the dirt at the roadside.

Then silence fell back over the desert again. Henry dropped the phone handset back into place and turned to Ottis with a grin and a hunger.

He took the other man there in the dirt by the roadside, roaring out the devil's secret names with every thrust, making Ottis into an offering just as surely he would this poor, simple girl that the Hands of Death cult had chosen as their latest victim.

Before the moon had fully risen fat above them, they were tearing off down the highway to the west, eager to fulfil the will of their master, bound to his demands, revelling in evil at his behest. No man could resist the will of Satan, so they could hardly be blamed for the things that they would do next or the sinful things they had done before.

'Stop.'

The sun had barely risen when they spotted the hitchhiker by the side of the road. She was the one. The one that their dark lord had chosen to be their next victim. She was the one that…

'Stop. Stop with all this devil worship nonsense. It doesn't make any sense.'

Henry's well-practiced recitation of his crime ground to a halt. 'What's that now?'

The detective on the other side of the table leaned forward to offer him another cigarette. They needed to keep the room good and smoky to cover up the unique reek that seemed to seep out of every one of Henry's pores. He'd been poisoned as a kid. That is what the prison doctors said. That was why he oozed that eye-stinging smell. It was the collective opinion of everyone on the force that a good wash would probably deal with most of the smell, but the medical eggheads insisted.

'The Satanism stuff.' The detective sighed. 'Nobody is buying it, Henry.'

Henry cocked his head to one side and scratched at his empty eye-socket. It wasn't easy with his wrist chains fed through the hoop in the middle of the table. 'What that you're talking about, now?'

'Nobody believes that you were sent on a mission by Satan to murder all these girls. I don't know who put this idea in your head that you'll get a lighter sentence if you bring the devil into it, but you won't. Just tell us the truth, and nothing but the truth. Okay?'

Henry looked genuinely perplexed. 'But the Hands of Death? What about them, huh?'

'Florida PD have been through the Everglades. They've gone to all the places that you said these cults had their meetings. There was nothing there. No sign of anybody. No human sacrifices. Nothing, Henry. It's just a fantasy, and I'm tired of hearing it.'

Henry wet his lips. 'All right, all right, all right.'

He took a moment to compose himself then launched back into his story as if he hadn't just been called a liar.

They pulled up alongside the hitchhiking girl, with twin alligator grins plastered across their faces. 'Hey now, what's a pretty little thing like you doing out here all by your lonesome?'

It was dark inside the car. She could see the shine of their grins but not the hunger in their eyes. She was upset, she needed somewhere to vent her frustration, and two friendly strangers seemed to be just the ticket. 'I just broke up with my boyfriend. I'm all done with men. They're the worst.'

'I would take offence, but I am inclined to agree with you there, Miss. I ain't never met a man, outside of my good buddy right here at my side, that I could stand for more than any length of time at all. Why I'd bet that boyfriend of yours isn't even worth spitting on if he's on fire.'

There was a strange charm to Henry, the same charm that had ensnared Ottis so easily and so deeply. He was like some old black and white movie star that had come out of the screen and roamed around. He was larger than life. People got caught up in his wake, and the whole world seemed to reshape itself around him. Nobody could charm a girl into a car like Henry. He was the gift that just kept giving, as far as Ottis could see.

The girl fell under his spell readily, bursting into giggles. 'Well, he isn't all that bad.'

Henry didn't even have to switch gears. As smooth as a Vegas hustler, he replied, 'I'm glad to hear you say that. As a matter of fact, because that boy of yours, I have to tell you, he is feeling mighty sorry for how he's crossed you. He stopped me and my buddy here and begged us, down on his knees begged us, to come out here after you and take you back to him. He knows he's done wrong, and he wants to make it right.'

'Wait'—a scowl crossed her face—'Kenny sent you?'

Henry chuckled, 'Well, I hope you didn't think I was in the habit of just stopping to chat up every pretty girl I came across at the side of the road. Of course Kenny sent us. He wants us to take you back to him so that he can make his apologies to you proper.'

It was hard to be suspicious in the face of Henry's overwhelming charm, but she still made the attempt. 'Why didn't he drive out here himself if he's so sorry?'

'Wouldn't you know it? That is a part of this sorrowful story, too. Your young man was all set to come a roaring out of town after you when he burst his dang tire. Nail right through it. That's how we met Kenny to start with, you see. We saw that poor boy pulled up on the side of the road trying to wrestle a jack under his car and, being the good Samaritans that we is, we hopped right out to help him. But would that boy hear of it?'

Ottis shook his head on cue. 'Nope.'

'No, he most assuredly would not. He said to us, "Don't you tarry here. I've got a girl out there in this merciless sun, and she needs rescuing. You good boys want to help me out? Then you get yourself back into that car of yours and you go find that girl of mine before she gets too far, because I've done wrong by her and I need to make it right."'

'That's what he said.' Ottis nodded along.

The girl dithered on the roadside. Henry was certain that she wasn't doubting his word, so the only alternative had to be that she was doubting her boyfriend. He leaned back in his seat. 'Listen here, Miss. I ain't got no attachment to your boy Kenny. If you tell me you never want to see him again, I'll give you a ride to wherever you've got to go to get away from him. I ain't even heard his side of things, only him hollering that he's sorry, so I don't know what sort of situation me and my buddy here just got wedged into the middle of.'

That seemed to cinch it. 'No. No, I'll go listen to what he's got to say. If nothing else, he owes me that apology.'

She opened the back door of the car and climbed in, wreathed in the smell of cigarette smoke and sweat.

'And this was on the twenty-eighth?' The detective interrupted Henry again, pen tapping on his clipboard.

'What's that now?'

'You picked this girl up on the twenty-eighth of August. Is that what you are saying?'

'Yeah, that's right. Of course. The twenty-eighth. Ottis strangulated her that afternoon. I fucked her. Then we buried her out by the rickety barn, right where I said you'd find her. You've dug her up, right?'

'Oh yes, we found the body exactly where you said it would be.' The detective nodded along. 'But here is the thing. You didn't kill her.'

Henry was getting angry. His empty eye-socket began to weep. 'I done already told you Ottis did the killing and I did the fucking.'

'I've got a pay-sheet from a job you were working on in Richmond, Virginia. Says that on the twenty-eighth you were roofing some old girl's house. How could you have been in two places at the same darn time?'

He took a long draw on his cigarette. 'What is this? You don't want my confessions no more?'

The detective sat back with a sigh. 'We want the truth, Henry. That's all we ever wanted. The truth.'

'Well, maybe that one was just Ottis then. Can't remember every little thing. You do enough of them and they all mix up. You remember every shit you ever took?'

The detective reached across the table and drew the packet of cigarettes out of the murderer's reach. 'Well, let's see if we can't jog that memory.'

The Son of a Whore

On August 23, 1936, Henry Lee Lucas was born onto the raw dirt floor of his family's log cabin in the backwoods of Blacksburg, Virginia. What would have been the cause for celebration in any normal family was an irritation and a serious imposition in the Lucas household.

His mother, Viola, was in her fifties but still working hard as the town prostitute, and every day that her genitalia were out of commission due to yet another unwanted baby was a day that the family was losing the pittance of money that she got paid for sex—typically, about ten cents per customer. It wasn't like his father, Anderson, was bringing much in to support his wife and the thirty-odd bastard children that she had spawned. While he used to make an acceptable living working on the railroads, his alcoholism soon cut that, and him, short. One night while blind drunk, he passed out on the tracks and a freight train rolled right over him, severing both of his legs. He survived the experience but spent the rest of his days in a little wooden wagon that he pushed around with a broom handle.

It was the last time that he tasted liquor. The moment that Viola became the breadwinner she asserted herself as the matriarch and master of the whole family, holding the purse strings of their extremely meagre fortune and using them as just another of her many tools to dominate and belittle everyone around her.

Even when Henry was a baby, his mother would pinch at him each time that he cried or fed. There was no kindness for Henry that didn't come with pain in equal measure. As soon as he was old enough to survive solid food, Viola put him down and never picked him up again. Affection was something to be purchased, not something freely given. But suffering—she had plenty of that to spare for her last-born son.

There was no plumbing in the cabin, no electricity either, just a wood-burning stove that Viola used to prepare meals for herself, her pimp, and very occasionally, her husband. Hot food was a luxury that little Henry would never experience. When she caught him trying to steal scraps from his father's plate one night, he was banished from the house to live in the chicken coop.

Henry was often seen gnawing on the woodwork of the coop as his teeth began to come in. He chewed off substantial amounts of the lead paint that coated it and, combined with the absence of any sort of cleaning routine, it wasn't long before he was suffering from several different types of poisoning—lead poisoning from the paint and cadmium poisoning from the chicken droppings and insecticide that was sometimes stowed away in there. By the time that he was old enough to walk, these poisons had already impregnated his body to such a degree that the smell of cadmium seeped constantly from his pores. By the time that he was old enough for school, the reek of it was enough to make his fellow students' eyes water. In the schoolroom he was seated beside an open window, no matter the weather, but even that wasn't enough to alleviate the stench—or the hatred that it instilled in the other students. Henry was loathed by teachers and students alike. He was completely isolated from the community in Blacksburg, with only the dubious company of his family elevating him from being a total pariah.

His parents—such as they were—remained more or less unreachable by the school or authorities, with any message that Henry carried back to them being discarded without a second thought. But eventually, one of the many demands that the boy be washed to deal with his ungodly smell finally made it through to Viola, and it sent her into a rage. She dragged the terrified boy out to the small pond bordering their property, stripped him naked and then held him under the water while she scrubbed and molested him in more or less equal measures.

'They wants him to be a pretty smelling little girl, then that's what we'll give them.'

She still had clothing from all of her older children stowed away for use as hand-me-downs, but one item held a particular pride of place amongst the belongings of all Henry's many half-siblings—a beautiful floral dress that had been intended for his older sister to wear to church. Viola forced Henry into it, then paraded him through town, bellowing, 'Look how beautiful my daughter is. I thought I had a son, but I guess that I was wrong.'

She marched him all the way through the school gates and into the building before scuttling back into the woods. Henry had to sit in the dress throughout the whole school day before he was finally allowed to run home, sobbing all the way.

It was far from the last time that he would wear that dress. It became one of Viola's favourite punishments for the boy to force him into girl's clothing. She had spent enough of her life at the mercy of men that having the opportunity to get some revenge on that gender was all too welcome. She loathed and feared all men, so being able to take the power away from them in any way was a massive thrill for her. She had long been using emasculation as a tool to control her husband. Every time she had a client come calling, she would prop her husband up in the corner of the room and make him watch. Soon, that disabled man was joined by what appeared to be a remarkably ugly girl. Henry was pinned in place by fear of his mother, repulsed and appalled by the things that she did for money. Whatever last embers of humanity might still have been burning inside of the boy despite all of the abuse that he had suffered died in that dimly lit cabin, watching man after man mount his mother and leave a few pennies behind in payment.

Henry was in desperate need of a friend. His older brothers had sensed their mother's particular antagonism to Henry, and they feared to suffer the consequences of seeming to be in cahoots with him. His father was wracked with constant pain, denied the alcohol that he had always used to numb himself before, and forced to watch man after man lying with his wife. He was completely lost in his own misery. If Henry ever came close, he lashed out at the boy with the broomstick he used to punt himself around.

There was nobody who could help to shoulder the unbearable burdens of his horrific childhood. No human being would have anything to do with him for fear of being dragged into the maelstrom that surrounded him, but he did find one creature in all of Blacksburg who seemed to care for him—a mule that he stopped to visit each day after school.

The nameless animal was the property of one of Anderson's old work friends, and it was serving no purpose lingering around his property. So when he discovered the delight that young Henry was taking in playing with the animal, he was more than happy to gift it to the boy.

Viola eyed the animal warily when Henry led it into their yard on a ragged rope. She didn't understand why the boy had brought it, and it took several rounds of vicious accusations before she calmed herself enough to listen to his fumbling explanation. She looked from the boy to the beast and back again, saw the affection in her son's eyes, the admiration of an animal that most would have overlooked entirely. The moment that she recognised it as love, she was consumed by jealousy. Viola loathed Henry, she wanted nothing to do with him even at the best of times, but she could not stand the idea of him finding comfort or love in anyone else, either.

Living on the fringes of civilization with domesticated animals of their own, the Lucas family needed a gun. It was very rarely used, and barely even thought of most days, but Viola could find it among the dark rafters by touch alone. The shotgun was kept loaded in case of emergencies, and the look in Henry's eyes, the softness and kindness there, that constituted an emergency in Viola's view.

She shot the mule, right in the face. Henry was sprayed with blood. It blinded him. With both hands, he wiped his eyes clean. He could feel a scream rising up his throat, but Viola's firm backhand cut it off before it could escape. 'What did you have to go and do that for? Now I've got to go and pay somebody to haul that useless carcass away, you worthless, stupid little rat-shit.'

She hit him again, an open-handed slap that dropped him to his knees with a gasp. There was blood on his hands. She kicked him in the ribs, hard enough to make them creak.

It was his fault. He shouldn't have loved that mule. This was what his love brought with it. Viola stamped on his hand as he held it up to her in desperate supplication. He'd been taught young that love came with pain, that joy came with a price. Why hadn't he listened? Why hadn't he learned?

Viola continued to punch and kick him until he was unconscious, then she dragged him back to the chicken coop to sleep it off. It wasn't the first time she'd beaten him like this, and it certainly wouldn't be the last.

The campaign of abuse that she inflicted on both Henry and his father to 'keep them in their place' was relentless. She insisted that both of them watch as she serviced her clients, sometimes dressing up Henry as a girl and threatening to rent him out alongside herself, sometimes just pushing them into one corner of the room so that they wouldn't disturb her 'gentleman callers' too much.

Henry never seemed to be numbed to that particular pain, no matter how many times he was exposed to the same routine. He would still flinch at the sound of flesh hammering into flesh, still struggle to keep the bile from climbing his throat. The first time he'd tried to run, Viola had been on him like a shot, like something out of a nightmare. Naked, bloated, and pale in the firelight, she'd dragged him back into the room by the ankles, and the man who'd paid to fuck her lay laughing on the bed as she kicked her son in the head.

After that, she'd gotten more creative in her punishments. She'd let him run, but every moment that he was out of her sight, his terror grew. He knew that she'd come for him when she was finished. He knew that the torments she'd inflict would be all the worse for him denying her immediate satisfaction. After she'd finished up her business, Henry would walk right back into the house for his beating, feeling every inch the helpless, terrified coward that she accused him of being as he wept and bled, begging her for mercy.

This violence reached its peak when he was just nine years old. Viola had set him the task of repairing the fence around the edge of their property, alone, and acquired some scrap wood in trade for her services. He laboured at this task all through the day, gladly missing school where he was treated like dirt, and finding some small measure of satisfaction in doing good work with his hands. His fixation on the task was so intense that when Viola called him, he didn't come running. She had a client waiting for her, already halfway to undressed in her bedroom, and Henry wasn't coming when called. The same old fury bubbled up in her. She rushed over to the wood stack, grabbed a two-by-four and swung for the back of Henry's head. The crack was so loud that they probably heard it in town, and he tumbled onto his face in the yellowed grass. Viola spat on him, then went back to her whoring without a second thought. That would teach the boy some respect; he'd wake up sore in the morning and regret even thinking of crossing her.

Night came and went, Viola's busiest working hours and drinking time all rolled into one. A few hours after sunrise, she climbed out of bed and went to the chicken coop to give the boy a piece of her mind now that he was conscious enough to hear it. There was no sign of him. With a snort, Viola turned on her heel and headed back to the cabin. 'Fool boy thought he could run away to school and be safe from her. Didn't he know that he just got it worse every time he ran? Little coward. Little idiot. Did he want to get beaten bloody?'

She was almost back to the house when she spotted the dew-covered lump out in the grass. Right in the same spot where she'd dropped Henry yesterday. Lazy little swine didn't even crawl back to his coop. She took a little run and then kicked him as hard as she could muster in the backside. Her ankle started to ache. 'Get up, you lazy little pig shit. You got a fence to finish.'

Henry didn't move a muscle. She kicked him again. Then again, hard enough that his limp body rolled right over and his slack-jawed expression was exposed to the morning sky. It was enough to make even Viola pause. With a tremor in her hands, she touched his face. He was cold. She moved her hands down to his lips and held them steady. His breath tickled over her fingertips, and the breath that she'd been holding herself came out in a whoosh. 'Get up, you lazy little bastard. Go on. Wake up.'

When it became apparent that Henry wasn't going to move under his own power, Viola set a couple of his older brothers to drag him inside and prop him up in the corner where he wouldn't get in the way. Anderson was parked in the opposite corner, utterly ignored by the swarms of children as they went about their day. Both of them forgotten.

Henry lay there for a day, forgotten. Then another. Viola had put him out of her mind. Anderson would have been powerless to help him, even if he hadn't been so lost in his own misery that he'd barely noticed the boy's state. Henry would have died there and then, on the dirt floor of that cabin, if it weren't for the most unlikely of benefactors coming to his rescue.

Viola's pimp, 'Uncle Bernie', had been coming and going as usual over the past few days, bringing her trade and returning for his cut of the takings, and he had noticed the injured boy.

Eventually, his basic humanity won out over his desire to stay detached from this horrid little family drama. He picked Henry up, tossed him in the back of his pickup truck, and drove him to the hospital.

Even a few minutes of concussion-induced unconsciousness is cause for medical concern, and Henry had been lying in an unmonitored coma for three days. The medical staff couldn't believe that the boy was still alive at all, and they certainly didn't expect him to ever regain consciousness after suffering what they assumed was extensive brain damage. It took a week before he regained consciousness, and when he did, it was alone in a strange, white place, completely unlike anything he'd ever experienced before. The people there spoke to him softly and kindly. Slowly enough that he never had to question them or doubt his own recollections. For the longest time, he thought he'd died and gone to heaven, but then the tests started in earnest. The needles and the endless questions.

What had happened to him? How much could he remember? When had he been exposed to cadmium? When had he been exposed to lead? What school did he go to? Who was the man who had brought him in? He couldn't even begin to understand some of those questions, let alone answer them. They took his dumbness in the face of questioning as a sign of amnesia or oxygen-deprived retardation. They accepted that accidents just happened sometimes.

When Uncle Bernie came back in to check on the boy, they could think of no good reason why he couldn't go home.

The seizures didn't come until later. Brutal, crushing things that Henry couldn't even remember afterwards. Every muscle in his body would contract, shaking and straining against every other one. His eyes would roll up into his head. He would froth at the mouth, let out little yips or screams. Back then, the doctors called them 'grand mal' seizures—violent convulsions that would wrack his whole body and leave him aching for days in their aftermath, even though he didn't even realise they'd happened.

One moment he would be fine, the next he would be flopping around on the ground, helpless and lost in the black static of his own brain.

After that harrowing experience, Henry shied away from his mother. Viola would have punished him for that before, beaten him bloody and tormented him even more, but at the urging of Uncle Bernie, who didn't want to see his meal-ticket going to jail for child abuse, she eased off on Henry.

With the obvious danger of calling down Viola's wrath finally gone, his half-siblings were delighted to welcome him into the family. The girls took pity on Henry, taught him how to wash properly, how to clean his clothes so that he wasn't so obvious a target for the school bullies. The boys, they were just glad to have a new playmate after so many years of stagnation. They would run, whooping and screaming through the woods around their house. They would rough-house, wrestle, swim in the creek, and hunt for squirrels until long after the sun had set and they had to trudge back to the never-ending misery of their parents.

By the time that he had reached the age of ten, in 1946, Henry was beginning to become as normal as it was possible for someone of his upbringing to be. He was starting to find some minor success at school, and the bullies who had plagued his early days eased off after they discovered—the hard way—that he carried a knife in his belt at all times, just like his brothers did.

Those knives were a daily part of the Lucas kids' lives. They used them to whittle crude toys for themselves out in the woods. They used them to skin the squirrels that they caught. There are a hundred small uses for a knife in rural life. Most importantly, though, they used them to fight. Not just with outsiders, but to settle arguments within the family, too. There wasn't a single Lucas child without a knife scar somewhere on their body, and as weak and starved as Henry was after his early years of neglect, he carried more of them than most.

Since his coma, Henry's movements were sometimes erratic and clumsy, like he had forgotten how his mind was meant to fit into his body. In the semi-playful knife fights of the family, this made him as much a danger to others as to himself, lurching around unexpectedly into harm's way.

It was during one of these playful little stabbings, on a sunny day in the forest, that Henry lunged forward unexpectedly, impaling his own eye on his half-brother's knife. The eyeball burst immediately, sticky vitreous sliding down his cheek and drawing a scream out of his brother's throat. Henry didn't scream. He didn't even shout. He seemed to be too surprised to even respond to the stimulus. He fell down to the ground as if he was going through the motions, then a seizure wracked him while his half-brother ran around looking for somebody to help drag him back to the cabin.

Viola took one look at her son, with blood and leaves caked to his face, and she shrugged. 'Ain't nothing to be done about it now. Just, don't be stupid again.'

His siblings did their best to wash out the now empty socket as Henry cussed at them all with surprisingly colourful language. As per usual, Viola had no intention of seeking out medical attention for her injured child, and with no frame of reference, the kids just went along with her. Somehow, despite a dirty knife inflicting the injury, soil and decomposing leaves getting rubbed into it, water from a stream being used to wash it out, and no hygiene being practiced by anyone involved, the injury did not get infected. Three weeks on from losing the eye, it was healing so well that the teachers at Henry's school assumed that it had actually been treated.

Henry had started to develop a little bit of a personality now that he was out from Viola's shadow. He had a wry sense of humour that passed most of the children his own age by but occasionally drew a chuckle from his teachers. He was far from being a favourite, and his presence was still more often than not a disruption in the classroom. But he was quiet and attentive, even if he couldn't get to grips with any of the more complex subjects. He left the teachers alone and they left him alone.

The same could not be said for all of his classmates. They were the usual mix of clowns and bored children that comprise most schoolhouse populations, and they received their fair share of punishment from their teachers as a result.

Henry was sitting one day, minding his own business and doing his best to be attentive to what his teacher was saying when the boy beside him started cracking jokes to a buddy. Henry paid them no attention either, but before long the constant guffawing had enraged their teacher. She turned and flung a ruler at the boy. She missed. The little slip of wood hammered into Henry's empty eye-socket and stuck there. All the noise that he'd never made when he lost the eye came pouring out of him now. He sounded like a pig being skinned alive. His teacher rushed over in a panic and tried to pull the ruler out, but it was stuck solidly in the soft tissue. She had to twist it to get it loose.

After that little incident, infection set in. Nothing life-threatening, nothing that would even impact his life too severely, but a persistent little culture of bacteria that would last for the rest of Henry's life, making his empty eye-socket weep milky tears at inopportune moments whenever he didn't have a glass eye in place.

Growing Pains

By the winter of 1949, the strain of living with Viola had become too much for Anderson. He had done his best to raise his children with some decency and dignity despite everything, but he had been marginalised so thoroughly by Viola that his lessons never took root. By the end, he simply whacked at his children with his broom handle whenever they came around to torment him. He had been reduced to less than a man—less than an animal—by their treatment, and he could have lived on for another twenty years in that same daily living horror if he hadn't had one brief moment of self-reflection. In the middle of the night, he dragged himself out of the cabin and into the snow. He kept on dragging himself forward for as long as he could, his atrophied muscles given new strength by the knowledge that there was an end in sight—that his suffering would soon be over.

That last desperate dash for freedom was a complete success. By the time the kids found him in the morning, he was already half dead from exposure. Even after he was taken to the hospital and pneumonia truly set in, he never regained consciousness.

By the spring of 1950, Anderson Lucas was dead and gone, and every attempt that he had made to instil values or restraint in his children were forgotten with him.

Puberty hit Henry Lee Lucas like the freight train that took his dead father's legs. He went from having no interest in the girls outside his family to having entirely too much interest in the course of a few weeks. He spent the summer of 1950 relentlessly pursuing every girl in his class and being quite brutally rejected by every single one of them in turn. He didn't have the social skills to navigate around his reputation around town, nor around his pungent aroma. The charm that he eventually developed wouldn't surface until a good few years down the line.

As a fourteen-year-old, the outlets for his sexual impulses were extremely limited, but once again, his brothers came to the rescue. They had spent many years hunting squirrels and rabbits in the woods around their cabin, but it was only now that Henry's sex-drive began to ramp up that he discovered why his older brothers still pursued such childish games. They were having sex with them. The same fate would probably have befallen his beloved mule if Viola hadn't intervened so early.

Henry took to his brothers' lessons so well that before long he was the one leading the hunt and expanding both the repertoire of animals that they would molest and the specific techniques that they used to maximize their pleasure in each case. It was Henry who discovered that slitting the throat of an animal just as he was approaching his orgasm led to it bucking around in a particularly thrilling way, and it was Henry who proved time and again that he was quite happy to go on fucking an animal after it was dead.

About this time, Henry's academic career came to its end. The woods were full of animals that were calling to him, his hormones were soaring, and he had no interest in any sort of work; not when his extended family had already turned his head to a far more lucrative way to spend his time. Cousins—kin of Viola for the most part—were forever passing through the Lucas house, with all of Anderson's family wisely distancing themselves from him after he made the fatal error of marrying her. And while not every one of them was a criminal or a drifter, enough of them were to leave a permanent impression on young Henry.

A series of burglaries started up across Virginia, mostly centred on Richmond, but extending well out in every direction. From scattered reports and sightings, it seemed like there was some roaming gang of teenagers and young adults hitting targets almost at random, taking very little care to avoid detection and trusting almost exclusively in luck to see them through. Still, no matter how far he roamed or how much money he managed to fence his goods for, Henry returned every time to Blacksburg and his mother's ever-waiting malice.

With money came better prospects for the boy. He was fifteen years old in 1951, as wealthy as he would ever be in his life, and learning some confidence for the first time thanks to the long periods of time that he was spending outside his mother's influence. Absence seemed to make the heart grow fonder, and many of the girls who wouldn't give him the time of day when they went to school together suddenly had an interest in the only boy their age who drove a car instead of a tractor. His interest in women was never romantic so much as it was an expression of his endless carnal desires, but he learned to play the game, at least a little. And the more that he acted like he was just interested in dating the girls that he pursued, the more success that he had with them—up to a point.

Henry devoted an inordinate amount of time and attention to wooing the girls that he pursued, obsessively attempting to purchase what he considered to be the natural conclusion to their arrangement. The girls, meanwhile, had been well-warned about the dangers of premarital sex, and the depths of depravity and destitution that it could lead to—often with the Lucas family being used as examples in the conversation.

After a month-long attempt at courting, interrupted only by his trips away to do a little breaking and entering, and the intricacies of keeping their relationship a secret from everyone in town, Henry came back to find the object of his affections just as reluctant to progress beyond heavy petting as she had been when he departed. Off in his car, deep in the woods, far beyond the usual spots around Blacksburg where necking teenagers usually haunted, he laid out an ultimatum. 'You either give it up to me like you're supposed to, or we ain't going to see each other no more. No more flowers, no more drives whenever you feels like it. No more nothing.'

Despite that persuasive argument, her knees did not part. 'I'm not like that, Henry.'

A tremor ran through him—not a convulsion but rage. After all he'd done for her. After all the money he'd spent. She wasn't like that? He'd make her like that. He'd make her so she was however he liked, whenever he liked.

He scrambled on top of her, his hands grasping, not for her chest, as she'd assumed, but for her throat. His hands shook as the corded muscles in his arms stood out. The girl didn't even have time to think, didn't have time to change her mind or to fight back. By the time she realised what was happening the world had already started to go dark. The last thing that she saw was Henry Lee Lucas looming over her, teeth gritted, eye-socket weeping with frustration and effort.

Once she was dead, he made swift work of her underwear, slicing it off and tossing it aside. He was intimately familiar with the mechanics of sex, having spent so much of his life with a front-row seat in a whorehouse, and it didn't take him long before he was happily humping away at the still-warm corpse.

With his urges sated, Henry looked down at the girl with disgust and regret; not that he'd killed her—he didn't care whether she was alive or dead—just that now he was going to have to deal with the body. He dug a shallow grave out by the fire road and tossed her in, still partially dressed. As he filled it in with dirt, Henry pontificated on the situation. Sex with dead girls was always going to be better because they couldn't say no to anything that you asked them. If he'd skipped straight to killing that bitch then he'd have saved himself a lot of work and money, and he'd still have got exactly the same thing in the end. It was just like fucking critters with his brothers. The thrill of the hunt adding a little edge to his arousal.

The killing did nothing for him, as it turned out. He knew some of his kin revelled in it—they had a real blood lust—but for him, it was as empty as any other act. A necessary step to get what he wanted, perhaps, but not something to be remembered or cherished. He cared so little about this girl, that when the time came to confess for his crimes, he couldn't even recall her name. Her body still lies somewhere out in the woods of Virginia, undiscovered in an unmarked grave or dug up and torn apart by scavengers. If her family missed her, there is no sign of it in the official records.

Later, Henry's account of this crime shifted. He described an entirely different set of circumstances, a completely different girl whom he had picked up at random from a bus stop, beaten unconscious and taken off into the woods to rape. He claimed that she awoke during the act of penetration, and tried to fight back, prompting him to choke her unconscious. Later still, he recanted both of these confessions claiming that he had never killed anyone at all.

The truth was always a moving target for Henry Lee Lucas, and with no body and no forensic evidence to examine, it is impossible to know which of the three versions of reality actually happened and which were spawned by deception and confusion. More recently, this confession has been linked to the disappearance of seventeen-year-old Laura Burnley, but no additional evidence has ever been produced to confirm that link.

Eventually, Henry's crimes caught up to him. Not the murder, nor the numerous sexual assaults that he had committed over the years before finally coming to his murderous revelation, but the petty theft that had been his only income. In 1954, he was convicted of several counts of burglary and sentenced to six years imprisonment. Rather than sending him to an adult jail and exposing him to the privations he'd be likely to face there, Henry was committed to Beaumont Training School for Boys.

It was not a successful placement. He was intensely disruptive and rebellious, and he seemed entirely incapable of absorbing any of the lessons that the school tried to instil in him. One of the staff later described him as 'a boy gone feral'.

Within a month, he made a successful escape from the institution, running all the way back to Blacksburg and the searing contempt of Viola. He had nowhere to vent his frustrations for the month inside that institution; nobody to be the recipient of his vile carnal interests.

One of his nieces, from an older half-sister, had been left in Viola's care. She was twelve years old and more than a little terrified of her wild-looking teenage uncle. That fear was well founded—he raped her out behind the chicken coop that had served as his home throughout his childhood, and threatened to slit her throat like a squirrel's if she said so much as a word about it to anyone.

Despite all the signs that he was a sociopath, Henry still clung to family as something sacrosanct. Despite all of the evil that he inflicted on them and that his mother had inflicted on him back in her day, he still wouldn't willingly kill his niece, even though their only connection was a tenuous one through genetics rather than any sort of bonding.

His well-thought-out plan of running away from the low-security prison may have gotten him home, but it was only a day later that he was picked up by the local sheriff and handed back over to the state. Once he had been committed to an adult prison, court proceedings went ahead and more years were slapped onto his sentence. But by that point, Henry didn't give a damn. Prison was heaven.

For the first time in his life, he had a bed of his very own. He got to eat hot meals for the first time, and he was guaranteed them, too, no matter whether he worked hard or not. There was no Earthly paradise for Henry that was sweeter than his time in that jail.

Where before he had only his family to educate him in the ways of crime, now he had hundreds of men, all arrested for a wide variety of crimes, with their expertise at his disposal. Even so, he didn't actively seek out any new criminal enterprises to indulge in, preferring instead to enjoy the good life while he could.

Even his appearance improved while he was imprisoned, with the doctors taking one look at his empty eye socket and immediately fitting him with a glass prosthetic to prevent the constant infections that had plagued him. In an instant he went from hideous back to merely unpleasant; some might even say rugged.

There are many men who indulge in opportunistic bisexuality when their environment demands it. Prisons, military forces, anywhere that there is segregation by gender, there are men or women finding love amongst their fellow captives. This was the case for Henry. While he'd shown a preference for women outside of prison, this was primarily due to a lack of education. He was not aware that men could have sex together, but once he had made that discovery, his little slice of heaven got that little bit more heavenly. Needless to say, he became extremely popular among his fellow inmates.

That popularity rippled out through the prison, and with his new friends and support network, Henry began to flourish, becoming a whole person for the first time in his life, developing a personality and a little bit of the charm that would serve him so well as time went on. He began to write to women through the prison pen-pal service, and while he lacked the artistry of some of his fellow prisoners when it came to pretty words, his honesty and almost child-like excitement to receive news from the outside world made him fairly popular in that regard, too.

By the time that he was offered early parole for good behaviour, Henry was actually well on his way towards being an at least partially reformed character. For the first time in his life, he believed that he could be somebody, that he could make something out of his life. As long as he was held out of the reach of his family, and more specifically the poisonous influence of Viola, Henry had a chance at living a real life.

The Dying Light

In 1959, at the age of twenty-three, Henry was granted early release and headed out into the world. Now that he'd experienced positive relationships, he had enough perspective to shy away from Viola on his own. Instead of trailing back to Virginia and the hovel that had been his home throughout his childhood, he went to stay with his half-sister, Opal, in Tecumseh, Michigan.

Henry had a great many relatives across the states, and despite everything that had happened in his life to date, almost all of them would have been quite willing to play host to him until he got back on his feet. Opal had never been much closer to Henry than any of his other relatives. Apart from being the girl for whom the dress he'd spent so much time in as a child had been bought for, they didn't have any special connection. Even so, she welcomed her little brother into her home with open arms and no questions about his plans and prospects for the future. He was hardly the first in their family to have spent a little time in prison, and he surely wouldn't be the last, so there was no judgement in that regard either. The fact that Opal worked long shifts at all hours certainly helped to make their cohabitation go smoothly, as did the disciplined cleaning habits that prison had instilled in him.

Even so, he had little intention of overstaying his welcome. There was already another home calling to Henry. The home of a woman who had already announced her willingness to be his bride in many letters before his release.

Stella was not a prize catch in the eyes of most of the population of Michigan. There was a reason that she had turned to the prisons of the world in her search for love. She was not considered to be a particular beauty, her personal habits sometimes verged on the odious, and she fully expected to rely on Henry to fuel her drinking habit once they were wed. None of that mattered to Henry. For the first time since he was a little boy, he had found someone to love; someone who seemed to love him back.

For the love of this woman, Henry was ready to turn his back on his criminal past, to set aside the horrors of his childhood, and to at least attempt to become a decent person. Prison had given him the freedom to become a better man, but in Stella, he found a reason to want to. He set about finding work in the city—real paying work rather than just another opportunity for crime. While he wasn't going to be winning anyone over with his employment history or skills, there were plenty of manufacturing jobs where intelligence and skills were pretty low on the list of priorities, which consisted of 'turns up to work at least fifty per cent of the time' and 'has arms to pull the levers.' Even the fact that he was a felon didn't count against him, as he had just enough sense to lie about where he'd been over the course of the past decade.

With his life on track, he made his play for the kind of normal life that had always eluded him, getting down on one knee in the Michigan snow and proposing to Stella after he'd picked her up for their regular date. With delight, she said yes, and they headed out to get thoroughly drunk to celebrate.

On his return home for the night, he shared all of his good news with Opal, who was delighted to hear that her little brother was finally getting his life on track. The very next morning, while he was still sleeping off the festivities, she started making rounds in the family to spread the joy.

When the news reached Viola, she was less than pleased that it had come to her via a third party, and even less pleased that Henry had been out of jail for weeks without even stopping by to inform her.

In the intervening years since Henry's arrest, life had taken a downward turn for Viola. After she shot a client in the leg with her shotgun for talking back to her, the trade from town finally began to slow. Her ever-advancing age did nothing to tempt Johns in, and even her longstanding arrangement with Uncle Bernie soon fell apart in the face of the economics of her declining appeal. In short, she was broke, unloved, and alone— not for the first time in her life, but certainly for the rest of her life. All of her children had gotten the hell out as soon as they were old enough to run from her, and they had scattered across the United States, some making it as far as the opposite coast in their desperation to escape her reach.

As she went into decline, Viola settled upon a course of action. She would need one of her children to come back and live with her, to pay for her and care for her in her advancing years. Preferably someone weak-willed with no real ties outside of the family. Someone she could browbeat and bully into subservience with the barest amount of effort so that she could get back to relaxing and enjoying the produce of Anderson's old moonshine still until death finally took her.

Naturally, her favourite choice for this joyless task was her youngest, and most broken, son. Henry getting his life together, neglecting what she saw as his duties and hiding from her all interfered with her plans. So, for the first time in many years, Viola left the old log cabin, went down into town, and boarded a bus for Michigan.

She arrived in Tecumseh just after nightfall on January 12, 1960, and it didn't take her long to track her daughter down. Opal was delighted to inform her mother that she had to go to work the night shift, and therefore wouldn't be around to entertain her, but old Viola made it excessively clear that she wasn't here to see her daughter anyway. Her sights were set on Henry. So, with only a little twinge of guilt, Opal sent Viola his way. Only a few minutes in her mother's company had been more than enough for Opal. But the way that she saw it, he was the one who had brought the old woman down on them, so he should be the one to suffer through her visit the most.

Henry and Stella were out at a bar when Viola arrived, having a proper, formal celebration of their engagement with her friends and his co-workers. The new Henry, the outgoing, happy Henry who was going places and making a life for himself, shrank back into the shell of the old Henry at her approach. He was struck almost mute as Viola stormed in, and it was only when Stella prompted him that he explained. 'Momma.'

Stella tried to greet Viola warmly, but she received nothing but a sneer in return. 'I ain't got no time for you. I'm here to see my boy.'

She pushed past Stella and took a hold of Henry's shirt. 'What're you thinking boy? What filthy little thoughts are sliming around in that head of yours?'

He couldn't even meet her eye. 'I'm getting married, Momma.'

'Ain't no woman ever going to marry you. You're scum. Girls would toss out their boots if they got you smeared on 'em. Nobody could ever love a dirty little bastard like you, Henry Lee. Not nobody.' She leaned in close enough that he could smell her foul breath. 'Not once I tell 'em all about what you did. Once they know what you are, ain't nobody is ever going to love you.'

For the first time in months, his missing eye began to weep. 'Momma, please.'

'Please? I don't remember you never saying please to me before. Don't remember you saying please to none of them animals or them children you put your dirty little pecker into, neither. Did you think I didn't know Henry? Did you think nobody knew what you were up to, you filthy little bastard? You monster!'

He wasn't sobbing, but water was streaming down both of his cheeks. 'Here is what you're going to do, Henry. You're going to say goodbye to your little whore here. You're going to pack up your shit. Then, you're going to get on the bus with me and we'll be going back home to where we belong. Wouldn't you like that, Henry? To come home like you was meant to when you got out of jail?'

Somewhere deep inside the crumbling husk of Henry Lee Lucas, that last dying spark of hope flared up. It drove him to stand up to his mother for the first time. 'No, momma. No. Stella loves me. We're getting married.'

From this close, Viola's shriek was almost deafening. 'No? You don't say no to me, boy!'

She started slapping him at first, then switched to closed fists when it became clear he was just going to cower and take it. 'You don't say no to me. You don't never say no to your momma.'

Her fists were a blur, blending the present moment with all the hundreds of beatings just like this that Henry had taken before. But then, suddenly, it stopped. Like an avenging angel, Stella had risen up between Viola and her prey. The two women were screaming at each other, shouting over the other. Neither woman getting an opportunity to get a word in edgewise. Still, Stella stood her ground, keeping her body between Henry and his mother like a shield. 'You can't treat him that way!'

Viola shrieked right back. 'Don't need no trash like you telling me how I can treat my boy!'

Then her fists were up all over again. If Stella had thought sanity or general decency were going to protect her from the wrath of Viola, then she was sadly mistaken. While there had been a grim fury on the old woman's face as she beat her son to the ground, it was now replaced with dark delight. This was what she had wanted from the very beginning. All that she had wanted was to come find the little bitch that would dare to take her baby boy away from her and knock her teeth out. It was like a dream come true.

She had knocked Stella to the ground and started kicking her before the bar's bouncer finally intervened, dragging the raving old woman out of the bar and ejecting her into the snow-covered street.

Henry rushed to his beloved's side and tried to sweep Stella up in his arms, but she pushed him away. She scrambled out of reach as his grasping hands came after her again. She was horrified to see this side of Henry. She had known some small part of his sordid history from their time as pen-pals, but she had no idea of the monster that had raised him, nor how powerless he was against her. With her hands still shaking, she stripped the engagement ring from her finger and threw it at Henry. She sobbed. 'I can't deal with this. That thing was your mother? That is what you came from? I can't marry you. This is just too much.'

Her friends swooped down on her, helped her back to her feet and formed a protective bubble of bodies around their fallen friend to keep Henry's grasping, begging, and pleading away from her. Somewhere in the press of bodies and the hubbub, Stella managed to escape him unseen.

To her friends, she said that she just needed some time to think things over. And after the initial shock had passed, it seems likely that she would have welcomed Henry back into her life. She would never get that opportunity, though. That train had already come off the rails, the passengers just didn't realise it yet.

He sat in the bar until they turned the lights out, drinking to numb the pain of his face and his heart, toying with his penknife the way that he always did when he was distressed. Flicking it open and shut with his thumb. He was blind drunk by the time they forced him into the streets, drunk and maudlin in a way that he wasn't accustomed to. He knew that he was sad about Stella leaving him, he knew he was sad about the way his mother treated him, but he didn't make the mental connection to the better life that he had planned for himself. He didn't understand that Stella being scared off by his mother was just the beginning of the death throes of his dream of a normal life.

He let himself into Opal's apartment without knocking. He knew that she was working all night, and it wasn't like any of the Lucas boys had ever had any trouble getting around a lock. He felt unnaturally heavy as he trudged to bed, like there was something huge and heavy hanging over him that he just couldn't see.

It was about a half-hour later that he woke to the steady drumming of a broom handle on his skull. Viola loomed over him like a nightmare that had followed him up from sleep. She was roaring and swinging for all that she was worth with the broom, and each blow set off fireworks in his half-drunk skull.

'Disrespecting me! Running around with some whore! Talking back to his momma!' Every bark punctuated with another strike.

He rolled out of bed trying to shield his head and scrambled past Viola into the living room as she went on raining blows all over his bare back. 'Momma, stop! Momma, stop!'

Begging had never worked before and it didn't start working now. Viola was relentless. She hit him with the broom until it snapped, then she switched to wild slaps. All of Henry's hopes and dreams were crushed under that flurry of wild swipes. She spat on him. Cursed him. Did everything that she could to remind him that he belonged in the dirt at her feet grovelling for attention. She could not see the man that he had become—in her eyes he would always be the snivelling little nothing, begging for her scraps. With each blow, she drove him back, drove him further and further inside himself until he began to believe it, too. Until there was nothing left of Henry except fear, pain, and despair. Until he finally reached the limits of his humanity and stepped over the precipice into raw animal instinct.

He didn't even notice his fist moving until it had already happened. It was a clumsy, wild swing that caught his mother in the neck rather than the jaw. Whatever he'd done was enough, though. Viola tumbled to the floor of the dark apartment, unconscious, or at least stunned long enough for Henry to make his escape. He bolted out of the front door without ever looking back or looking down. If he had, he might have noticed that his penknife was still in his hand, sticky with blood, and that he'd fallen asleep before folding it shut again.

He ran out into the street, hotwired the nearest car, and fled Michigan, still half-dressed and wild with terror.

Regressed as he was to his childhood state by Viola's last round of abuse, it should come as no surprise that he reverted to the behaviours of childhood, too. He knew he'd done something wrong, even if he couldn't fully grasp the magnitude of his own actions. He knew that his mother was going to be furious and that delaying would only ensure that his punishment was so much worse than it had to be.

Henry drove through the night, all the way back to Blacksburg, Virginia. He fled all the way back to the cabin and squatted down on that dirt floor, sobbing and waiting for his mother to come home and punish him. Cowering in dread, but certain that this was the right thing to do. That his being here would please his mother. That she might go gentle with him because he'd done this to placate her fury.

He was there for a full day before he realised that something was wrong. But even so, he crept out of the cabin cautiously, fully expecting her wrath to descend on him the moment he stepped out into the sunlight. She must be waiting for him to come back to Opal's apartment. He felt so stupid for thinking she'd come here instead of staying put. Stupid, stupid, stupid. Just like she'd always said he was. He climbed back into his borrowed car and started the long drive back to Tecumseh, but he only made it as far as Toledo, Ohio, before the local sheriff pulled him over on an outstanding warrant. It was only once they'd secured him properly that they told him what he was even being arrested for. The murder of Viola Lucas.

Their version of the story was repeated to him in excruciating detail to force his confession. After his mother awoke him in the middle of the night to continue the argument he had started back in the bar, he had taken his knife—the knife that he still had in his possession when they arrested him—and stabbed her in the throat with it. She had not died quickly. In fact, the tiny cut that he had inflicted had barely even nicked the artery. The blood had not drained from her body in a great rush. It had trickled out drop by drop while his mother lay abandoned and alone on the floor of a strange apartment in a strange city. It took all night for her to bleed to death. But by the time Opal had returned home from her long night shift, it was over.

At first, Henry tried to explain that he hadn't known the knife was open, that he'd forgotten it was in his hand but that story was too dubious to even justify a response beyond contempt. Next, he tried to argue that it was self-defence, and the forensic evidence certainly supported that interpretation to a degree. Henry was covered in bruises, the broken broom handle was found lying just out of Viola's reach, and her history of violence could certainly be taken into account. But nobody could believe that a young, healthy ex-convict in his physical prime could not prevent a woman in her seventies from attacking him without resorting to murder.

In Michigan, he stood trial for his crime, and the jury was even less inclined to believe his pleas of innocence than the police had been. They did not believe the prosecution's claim that the murder was premeditated, but they absolutely believed that Henry intended to kill Viola when he hit her. Some guilty part of Henry had to admit the truth in that sentiment, too. In that moment, as much as he loved his mother, he had wanted her dead. She had taken everything from him, and now, in one final act of spite, she took his freedom. He was sentenced to forty years imprisonment, eligible for parole in twenty. They had to carry him out of the courtroom, a broken husk of a man headed for Southern Michigan State Prison.

A Boy Named Sue

On March 5, 1947, another boy was born in barely more fortuitous circumstances. Jacksonville, Florida, was not the sterile sprawl that it would one day become in 1947. Beyond the reach of the central city hub, where all the traffic ran through, there were still communities living uncivilised lives within easy reach of the urban amenities. The Toole family lived in what would now be considered suburbia but was then just another development thrown up hastily and haphazardly to contain the latest influx of rural settlers hoping to escape their lives of poverty, and finding instead a whole new life of poverty waiting for them. Money was tight and liquor was plentiful—in short, it was a powder keg.

Ottis was not the healthiest child, suffering from severe epilepsy that sent him into grand mal seizures at the drop of a hat. After years of these seizures, a doctor eventually got involved, diagnosing the epilepsy but offering nothing in the way of treatment or preventative measures. An IQ test was administered to the boy at the time of examination, and he was discovered to have a mild mental disability, likely a result of brain damage following his seizures.

With the poor understanding of epileptic fits at the time, there were murmurs among the more religious fringes of the community that the boy was possessed. But pursuing an exorcism or any other kind of religious intervention would have required either one of his parents to give a damn about him.

From a very young age, Ottis's mother made it clear that she had wanted another daughter and had no use for a son. She dressed him almost exclusively in hand-me-down dresses from his older sisters, referred to him in public as a girl, and called him Susan at every opportunity.

Susan was by far not the prettiest girl in the Toole household, but she was the most defenceless. When Ottis's father entertained the other neighbourhood alcoholics, it was that five-year-old boy who was forced to tend them while his older sisters stayed well out of the way, fearful of the filthy old men and their groping hands. If he hadn't been wearing a dress the whole time, it is possible that they wouldn't have troubled him. If his father hadn't seen dollar signs the first time that a hand went up the boy's skirt to fondle him, the whole course of Ottis's life might have changed. But he did, and it wasn't. Ottis's father rented him out to his friends for a few cents a turn. It didn't matter how Ottis screamed or slapped at them. They were deep in their drink and the screams just added to their excitement.

After that first night, Ottis's father tried to prostitute the child again, but in the cold light of day, all of the drunken rapists saw their actions in a new light. Every once in a while, he would find someone new in town with the right proclivities, but Jacksonville was just a stop on the highway for most people—there wasn't a lot of return custom.

Despite the infrequency of his prostitution, the knowledge that 'Little Susie' had been a whore completely changed the already abusive familial relationships that he had. He was treated like filth by his devout mother like it was his fault that men had held him down and raped him while his father laughed. News travelled fast around the neighbourhood, and the girls who had once looked on him as an oddity and a cause for pity now considered his enforced cross-dressing to be a sign of depravity. Sexual assault and molestation became an everyday occurrence, not just by a couple of the neighbourhood men who had that inclination but also by the girls, including his sisters and mother who would grab at him under his skirt while making disparaging comments about his manhood.

One day, while fleeing from this horrific treatment, Ottis ran out onto the porch of the family home, even though it had been disused for many years due to rot. His weight was just enough to punch through the sodden wood and he fell right onto his face. In itself, this would not have been a memorable moment of misery in Ottis's life—pain was not unusual to him. What was unusual was the exposed nail that the fall had driven right through his skull, two inches into his brain. His mother pulled it out without thinking twice, and suddenly his usual seizures became much more frequent.

Ottis's father left one day without a word to anyone, one spring evening in 1957. He had been an alcoholic for years and a travelling salesman for longer, so it wasn't all that much of a surprise to anyone involved. He'd always drunk more than he made, so there wasn't a financial strain involved in the abandonment. But without his calming influence, Ottis's mother became more and more zealous in her persecution of the boy on a religious basis. It is likely that this would have reached a lethal conclusion if it weren't for the intervention of a more powerful figure in the family cosmology than God himself: Ottis's grandmother.

Where others saw his fits and sexual history as signs of demonic influence, Ottis's grandmother saw... exactly the same. But while to the Christian community of Jacksonville this was considered to be a terrible thing, his grandmother and her fellow Satanists took it to be a blessing.

She took Ottis under her wing, calling him her 'Devil-Child' and curbing the worst of his mother's excesses with the application of some good old-fashioned fear of the devil. She dressed him in boy's clothing, embraced his oddities as signs of infernal intervention, and cared for the boy in her way. With that care came a new set of obligations for the child. No longer did he have to serve as a house servant in his mother's paltry home. He had a higher calling now, and a far grander master to perform for.

There is a great deal of debate about how much of Ottis's reported childhood of satanic rites actually occurred, and how much was conjured from his fevered imagination. The self-mutilation that he later described was certainly corroborated by the patterns of scars on his body, and there were many reports of grave-robbing that line up neatly with his described activities. But the stories of human sacrifice that he claimed to have witnessed and the cannibalistic feasts—an inversion of the Catholic sacrament—have no evidence to support them. There were certainly missing people around Jacksonville at the time, and it is possible that some of them fell under the blade of some cultist, but it is just as likely that these stories were mere inventions of Ottis during one of the phases when he was trying to concoct a greater meaning to his actions; much greater than simple hedonistic pleasure.

Puberty hit Ottis hard and it hit him early. By the age of twelve, in 1959, he began showing hints of stubble, and he was forced to admit that he was indeed different from the other boys, who were now no longer a source of fear and confusion for Ottis and had instead become the cause for unexpected arousal.

Never one for lying, Ottis was honest with his family about his burgeoning homosexuality, even talking a little with his sisters about a boy whom he had been maintaining a relationship within the neighbourhood. The news was not well received. The fervour with which his mother had tormented him in his early years returned threefold. He was beaten at every opportunity on the most spurious of evidence, and before long he began to sleep in abandoned buildings rather than take the risks that came with returning home.

There were no shortage of abandoned houses in Jacksonville, with the rural families trying to start over discovering rapidly that opportunity did not await them there, so Ottis had little trouble finding places to stay in night after night. The only thing that troubled him in the beginning was the cold. It took him longer than he would have liked to admit to work out how to build a fire in the houses where he slept, but even once he had worked out the basic mechanics of it, he was still sloppy. Less than a month after setting his first fire, he lost control of one and it burned down the house where he had intended to spend the night.

Something in his brain clicked at the sight of that fire. It was like the flames were the catalytic agent that his burgeoning sexual awakening required to complete its formation. He began to set fires more frequently, more deliberately. He became aroused when he set those fires, and before long, every house that he slept in went up in smoke the next morning. The fires became the reason, more than his safety, that he slunk around abandoned houses at night.

By 1961, at the age of fourteen, Ottis had abandoned any hope of living a normal life. All of his days he had been called a freak, a deviant, a monster, and he had never seen any evidence to the contrary. He dropped out of school, where his contributions were barely missed, and began a career of extremely petty crime: selling along salvaged goods from abandoned houses before he torched them, panhandling, and eventually offering his services as a prostitute.

There were few gay bars in Jacksonville, but the fourteen-year-old Ottis became a regular at every single one of them. Initially, it wasn't out of a desire for trade, it was out of a desire for companionship. He desperately wanted someone like him, someone who could understand what he was going through. Instead, the men took one look at him and judged him. He was poor, a little bit dirty, in a way that wasn't entirely unappealing, and there was only one thing that a boy like that could have been after. They might not have been able to offer him the understanding he so desperately craved, but sex and cash were readily available. Ottis took what he could get.

There was a small gay community in Jacksonville, but a disproportionate percentage of that population was comprised of male prostitutes, thanks to all of the travellers passing through. While they didn't appreciate the extra competition that Ottis presented, they weren't made of stone. When the confused boy found his way into their care, they did what they could to keep him right. The local gay scene didn't like to see its members preying on the community, so it wasn't long before Ottis learned to pick up his clients from truck-stops and the like rather than lingering in bars. He made a clear division between his working life, where he had sex with travellers out by the roadside, and his extremely tenuous social life spent drinking and flirting in the gay bars in town.

One night, Ottis was picked up by a travelling salesman. That was enough to make him uncomfortable in itself, tangling up with his memories of his father's abuse, before the situation had even begun to develop. Not all of Ottis's clients were particularly kind to him, or even complimentary, but he was very rarely frightened for his life. This client was different. The moment that he got Ottis into the car, he tore off down the freeway without a moment's pause, laughing all the way. In the middle of nowhere, ten minutes out of town, he swerved off the road and slammed on the brakes, flinging the unsecured Ottis into the dashboard and knocking the air out of his lungs. He dragged the dazed boy out of the car and forced him down onto all fours in the glare of the headlights. There was no pause for preparation, no hint of humanity at all. He raped Ottis, taking delight in the boy's screams and sobs. 'Go on, yell. Nobody is going to hear you out here.'

When he was finished, the salesmen tossed a handful of change onto Ottis's prone form and staggered back towards his car, fumbling with his trousers and laughing all the way. He stopped in front of the car to light a cigarette and looked back at the night's prey with another little giggle. He stopped laughing abruptly when he realised that the boy was gone. He turned and made a dash for the driver's side, but Ottis got there first. Blood, and worse, trickled down his bare legs to stain the upholstery as he slammed the door shut, but he didn't give a damn.

Ottis slammed the car into reverse, then hammered it forward into the salesman with as much acceleration as he could muster. The thump of the impact would have been loud enough to alert people for a mile around, but the salesman had made sure that they were somewhere that nobody could hear them. Ottis reversed back over the man and got the car back up to the side of the road. He got out to retrieve his trousers and to check that the salesman was dead. He was. His skull had been crushed to a pulp. Another man might have spat on his rapist, but a darker passion than vengeance had enveloped Ottis. He reached down and masturbated over the corpse of his first victim until he had, what he would later describe as, the best orgasm of his life.

With that done, he took whatever cash he could find, got himself dressed, and drove back to the edge of town before abandoning the car in one of the hundreds of disused lots—his first murder complete, and the connection between killing and sex firmly cemented in his mind. The last puzzle piece of sex, pain, and fire finally slotting into place: death.

For almost a full three years, Ottis lived the life of a vagrant teenage prostitute, sleeping in a different abandoned house each night, staying well clear of his family, in particular his grandmother, who still held an almost unnatural sway over him. It is entirely possible that he could have gone on living like that on the fringes of Jacksonville forever if it hadn't been for a state governor who had decided that being hard on crime and immorality was going to secure him the votes he needed for an upcoming election.

The seventeen-year-old was arrested by plainclothes police during a sting at one of his regular pickup spots in August of 1964. They couldn't prove that he was engaged in prostitution, primarily because the evidence that they often used to convict prostitutes was possession of prophylactic devices such as condoms, and Ottis lacking any sex education beyond the mechanical had never even heard of them. He received six months in jail for 'loitering with intent,' even if they couldn't prove what that intent might have been.

Much like Henry Lee Lucas, Ottis found that his time in prison was far from the punishment that he had imagined it might be. He didn't have to work for his supper, and the only sex that he was having was fully consensual, which was more than he could ever have said before. Most importantly, his imprisonment severed any ties that he still had to the community in Jacksonville and filled him with new confidence that he could survive outside of his family's shadow.

When he was released, Ottis had the whole world at his feet, nothing to tie him down, and the whole of America as his backyard. He stole himself a car from just a couple of streets away from where the prison bus had dropped him off and set out to explore this brave new world. Drifting, panhandling, and prostituting his way across the southern states, under the radar of law enforcement, and slipping between all official records for years.

Making the Perfect Killer

Henry Lee Lucas was in a pit of despair when he returned to prison for the second time. Jackson State Penitentiary in southern Michigan was everything that his first prison had not been: filthy, underfunded, and full of men driven past the edge of reasonable behaviour by their circumstances. Fights were frequent, overcrowding was prevalent, and Henry, lost in his own thoughts, did nothing to take the initiative and establish a place for himself in the ecosystem.

All of the progress that he had been making towards a normal life was in tatters; any hope that he ever had of humanity had been stripped away. Whether he had killed his mother by accident or with intention was irrelevant—he was still the man who had killed his own mother. The rest of his family had been surprisingly quick to forgive him—either because they believed his story of accidents and self-defence or because they were simply glad that the monstrous woman was finally out of their lives—but the one person who could never forgive the crime was Henry himself. Viola had taken very little time to instil values in Henry, but the one that had been hammered home time and again was the importance of respecting and obeying your parents. Henry had broken the one sacred rule that had ever been given to him and he could not live with the terrible shame.

His first suicide attempt was very nearly a success. He fashioned a noose for himself out of his bedclothes and hung himself in his cell for almost twenty minutes before a patrolling guard noticed. The makeshift rope had not been tight enough to properly cut off the blood supply to his brain, just interrupt it badly enough to render him unconscious, and possibly add a little to the extensive brain damage that he had already suffered. The injuries were minor enough that the doctor didn't even report the suicide attempt—too much paperwork and too much effort all around setting up a watch for some nobody.

Henry was returned to the general prison population, went through the motions obediently to keep the guards happy, and about two months later, when he had recovered his strength and he was certain that nobody was watching him, he tried it again. He got the rope right the second time around, the sheets twisted tight enough to bite right into his neck, to knock him out instantly instead of the agonising, lingering gasps for air that the first suicide attempt had brought. What he hadn't accounted for was a changed guard rotation. He was only dangling for two minutes before the guards found him and hauled him off to the medical block. This time, there was no question about reporting it. It had gone from one foolish mistake to a pattern of behaviour, and a pattern of behaviour meant that Henry Lee Lucas could be foisted off on some other overcrowded government-run facility instead of remaining their persistent problem.

The recipient of this burden would be Ionia State Mental Hospital. It was there that the complex web of misery that comprised the mental state of Henry Lee Lucas finally came under some scrutiny. When asked about his suicide attempts, he eventually admitted that he had heard his mother's voice telling him to do it. Day and night. Even in death, Viola would not leave her son in peace. There was no prescription for guilt or ghosts available in Ionia State. Nor was there any real way to help a patient who had been raised from birth to keep every detail of his life a secret for his own protection, someone with a history of criminality so brutal that divulging secrets in therapy would likely lead to the death sentence or life imprisonment. All that they could do was treat that sole symptom, the hallucinations, as though it were the sum of his problems.

He received an extensive regimen of sedatives to keep him calm and compliant during the rest of his therapy, and for what the doctors termed 'schizoid delusions' he received weekly electro-convulsive therapy. In essence, triggering the grand mal seizures that had plagued him since childhood in the grim hope that eventually he would wake up with his brain 'reset' to normal.

With his brain damage suitably aggravated by the electrocution, and the more aggressive elements of his personality more or less entirely suppressed by the medication that he was on, Henry became one of the favourite patients of the staff. They soon recognised the spark of intelligence still burning in Henry, carefully tempered by the haze of sedation, and set him to work in the filing room, organising the files of the other patients. The hospital was home to some of the worst criminals in the local states. Those who had committed crimes so grievous that they were considered to be beyond the actions of the sane. A full account of every one of their crimes was contained within the files that were handed over to Henry, along with a full explanation of all the holes in the criminal justice system that these criminals had been able to slip through, ensuring that their crime sprees could continue long beyond the point that logic would suggest that they could be stopped.

Sitting alone in the stuffy file room for days on end, Henry got an education in how to avoid detection and capture; a masterclass from some of the world's most despicable criminals and most competent law enforcement. He discovered that moving from one state to another could completely stymie an investigation as the different departments failed to communicate properly. He discovered the various means of countering forensic investigation, by destroying the body of a murder victim or moving them around to rob the police of corroborating evidence. Ultimately, he learned that patterns were the enemy of every mass murderer. Using the same methods to hunt victims. Using the same methods to dispatch them. These were the amateur mistakes of lesser killers who soon got caught. By moving around, by destroying evidence, by switching the mode of murder, Henry slowly realised he could go for years without the police ever drawing any connection between his crimes. So far, he had committed two murders, and only the one, where there was an obvious and direct familial connection, had ever caught up with him. Randomised victim selection was added to his list of methods to avoid capture.

At this point, all of this was entirely academic. He had no intention of committing any further crimes. Indeed, by the time that he was released from prison, he expected that he would be too old to pursue any of the pleasures that had once formed the backbone of his existence. His sentence to forty years imprisonment had not been lessened by his transfer to the hospital. If anything it had been lengthened. Now, he would not be free until he was judged by the medical staff to no longer be a danger to himself and others—something that Henry knew in his heart would never happen.

He was, at his core, a killer. Now that he had a few years to think about the death of his mother, he accepted that his part in it was no coincidence. He had always had the instinct to kill buried underneath the mesh of terrors that had been his childhood. The fact that it had only come to the fore a couple of times in his life was more thanks to a lack of opportunity and luck on the part of his potential victims than on any sort of restraint. He had broken the only rule that had ever been laid down for him and walked away from it without consequences. He was truly free to do whatever he wished. If it weren't for the constraints of imprisonment, he had absolutely no doubt that he would kill again, and again, and again; for his own amusement, for his own advancement, maybe even just for the sake of seeing someone die.

It was a small comfort to him that he was never going to be faced with making the decision of who lived and died. At least until ten years into his sentence, when he was suddenly informed that he was being released.

'There's got to be a mistake. I ain't even up for parole for another ten.'

The doctor looked up from his clipboard, calm and assessing. 'There is no mistake, Mister Lucas. This facility is suffering from severe overcrowding, and you have shown a remarkable recovery in your time with us. Provided that you continue with the regimen of medication that is prescribed to you, I can see no reason that...'

Henry interrupted. 'I'll kill again. If you let me out of here, I swear I'll do it.'

'Mister Lucas,' the doctor sighed, 'you have shown no indication of any schizoid behaviours since undergoing your therapy, and it seems quite clear that the circumstances of your crime were... unique, to say the least.'

'No, doc. They weren't. Ain't ever going to be a shortage of necks and knives. If you send me out there, why, I'll leave a body on your doorstep.'

The doctor finally looked uncomfortable under his thin veneer of professionalism. 'Regardless of your feelings on this matter, I'm afraid that the decision has already been made, at a higher pay grade than mine. Tomorrow morning you will walk out of here a free man, Mister Lucas. I suggest you use this time to say your goodbyes to any friends and to turn your mind to more positive avenues. Consider profitable ways that you could make use of your freedom. The ways that your newfound clarity might help others.'

His psychological profile listed off a wide variety of symptoms that could have been tied to just as many different disorders, but the majority of his issues were attributed to head trauma alone—indeed, one psychologist said that Henry was fundamentally healthy except for being 'exceptionally needy' as a result of his childhood neglect.

The very next morning, on August 22, 1970, with crushing inevitability, Henry was released. This is, once again, where the reality that he described in his confessions and the reality that could be proven, diverge. Within sight of Ionia State Mental Hospital, Henry would later claim to have met two girls, pretty teenagers of the sort that he had always preferred. He took them somewhere private, plied them with liquor and strangled them, one by one, while the other was distracted and insensible. He took his time, having sex with their dead bodies through the night, then stole himself a car and drove out of town the next morning. No evidence can be found of this double homicide, and Henry later recanted his confession, but once again, there were a great many missing persons cases in the area that went unsolved. It isn't outside the realm of possibility that he committed these crimes and hid the evidence with sufficient skill that the bodies were never discovered. After all, he had just spent ten years studying criminology.

It would have made sense at this point for Henry to vanish entirely, to drift, as Ottis Toole had chosen to do, and to use his new specialised skills to gratify all of his darkest urges, but there was still one tie binding him to humankind. His family tree stretched out like kudzu across America, massive and complexly tangled. In this time of uncertainty, it was them that he turned to. For the next few years, Henry attached himself to his various cousins, uncles, half-brothers, half-sisters, and in-laws like a lamprey, living off each one for as long as they would tolerate until they eventually drove him off. It became a running joke in the family, with a warning call being sent out to all nearby relatives every time Henry was excised from one household that he would soon be on his way to another. Henry wasn't exactly loathed by his family. He had a pretty good temperament compared to the majority of the Lucas clan, he was relatively charming and provided that he was never left alone with anyone's children, there was never a problem. There was always one sure-fire way to be rid of Henry when the time came. All that anyone had to do was mention the death of Viola to stun him into sullen silence. He'd move on shortly after being reminded of his mother, without fail.

In 1971, he tangled with law enforcement once more, firstly for attempting to pick up a fifteen-year-old girl in his car, using a spiel about her boyfriend being angry at her to try and trick her into the vehicle. When that failed, she told the police about the incident and they promptly picked him up, only to discover that he was in possession of an illegal pistol; a violation of his parole. This earned him a fresh four-year stint in a Michigan prison. For Henry, this was a return to form, a little jog of his memory about just how comfortable regular hot meals and an actual bed could be. It was enough to convince him that he might like to settle down for a time. He turned to the prison pen-pal system all over again, finding an inexplicably willing woman named Betty in Port Deposit, Maryland.

It took him quite some time to discover exactly what was wrong with Betty. Nobody looking for love behind bars was doing so because they had a buffet of options in the outside world. But unlike Stella, Betty did not seem to be one of the dregs of society like Henry. Eventually, she admitted to having two pre-teen daughters. But if she had expected that to put off her new beau, she was sadly mistaken. He enquired after the girls extensively, restraining himself enough that his interest seemed to be parental rather than prurient. Betty thought that she had finally found herself a keeper.

In 1975, Henry had finished his sentence, and within only a few hours of his release, he was on a bus to Maryland and the waiting sofa of his cousin Wade, who lived conveniently just a short drive from Port Deposit.

Betty was smitten with her new husband-to-be, and it took no time at all before Henry had secured himself a job at the local scrapyard, where it turned out all of his years breaking into cars had given him all of the vital skills required to break them down into their valuable component parts and even to rebuild them, ensuring enough stability that Betty was willing to commit when he asked her to marry him.

Without Viola's interference, planning rushed ahead and the ceremony—well attended by the Lucas clan's local branches—was conducted on December 5th of that very same year. The happy couple and Henry's two newly acquired stepdaughters moved into a reclaimed mobile home in Lot C3 of Benjamin's Trailer Park in Port Deposit, Maryland.

Things started out quietly enough for Henry and Betty until he discovered that by driving around using his wrecker tags he could completely circumvent the DMV and police detection. That was when Betty found that he would go missing for days at a time, returning reeking of booze and the faint hints of perfume. She assumed that if he was philandering, some word would work its way back to her through the gossip network of the town. But whatever women Henry was going off with must have just vanished afterwards, because not a single rumour ever made it back to Betty.

Henry wasn't a perfect husband in any respect, but his drinking was usually reasonable. He paid for everything, he never lifted a hand to Betty, and he was fairly charming. The only thing that sat wrong with her was the way that the girls seemed to have chilled to him all of a sudden. In the beginning, the prospect of a new dad had been the cause of great excitement, and Henry had been almost overbearing in the kindness that he lavished on them. Gifts had been well received, but the attention had been what they were really craving. After so long with no father and a mother working long shifts to support them, Henry's open adoration of the girls had meant the world to them. Until suddenly it didn't.

She didn't know what she was looking at. She had no basis for comparison. Even when she realised that something was wrong, Betty couldn't put the pieces together, until one awful morning when she went to change the girl's sheets and saw the tell-tale silvery stains, rust-speckled by her daughters' blood.

Henry was late home that night, with the faint aroma of bourbon clinging to his lips when he tried to press them to Betty's cheek. She didn't raise a hand to him—she still didn't dare risk anything of the sort after the years of beatings from her first husband—but she pulled away and couldn't bite back the words that hissed out between her teeth. 'You bastard.'

Henry just smiled, the way that he always did, disarmingly and softly as a kiss. 'Now what am I meant to have done wrong this time?'

'I know what you done, Henry.' Betty was not charmed. Her voice was cold as ice. 'There's no question about what you done. I'm just trying to decide what to do about it.'

Her old husband had a look about him when he was about to start yelling. His eyes would narrow, his face would go red. Henry wasn't like that. He hardly raised his voice at all if truth be told, but in those moments when she'd seen him riled to anger it, was invisible. Whatever expression had been on his face before stayed plastered there like a mask while he acted out his fury. Even this close, Betty couldn't tell if he was insensible with drink, genuinely puzzled, or readying himself to knock out her teeth. The mystery of him had been appealing in the beginning, but now, nearly a year since he'd come out of that prison and into her life, it grated at her. He could have been thinking anything and she'd never even know.

His voice was almost unnaturally soft when he finally replied. 'I ain't got a clue what you're talking about, and I'll bet you ain't got a clue neither.'

It wasn't a threat exactly, just a statement of how Henry wanted the world to be. A broad accusation like Betty had just laid down would have had the mind of any normal person scrambling through all of the little secrets that they kept, trying to work out which one they had to protect. Henry was not so divided in his purpose. Every one of his secrets was enough to earn him a life sentence or worse. The only question on Henry's mind was the level of response that was going to be necessary.

'You've been touching my girls. You've been going in their rooms at night and...' She cut off in a strangled sob.

The tension in Henry loosened just a little. Was that all? That was hardly worth making a fuss over. 'I ain't never done nothing like that, Betty. I'd never lay a hand on either one of them girls. Swear on my mother.' If that was meant to be ironic, Betty would never know.

'I saw the...' She trailed off with a shudder. 'I spoke to the girls. They told me what you done. There's no point lying about it now. I know, and pretty soon everybody else is going to know, too. I'm going to tell the whole world that Henry Lucas touches little girls.'

There was another moment of his odd stillness. He then seemed to settle on a course of action. 'Now listen here. If you had enough with me, then that's fine. You just say the words and I'll pack up my bags. But don't go telling folks no lies about me just to drive me out. You want the trailer? It is all yours. But don't never go telling lies about how I touched them girls of yours. I took care of them like they was my own, and I don't know what sort of dirty stories you been planting in their heads, but I ain't going to sit here and listen to this.'

She was crying, gently, but maybe this was what was best for everyone. 'You better get out of here, Henry. I see you 'round here again, I'll tell everyone. I'll call the police. You hear?'

'I got my family reunion down Virginia way this weekend.' Henry was still speaking softly, still working the thought through. 'I'm going down there with Wade. We'll be gone a few days. Maybe that'll give you some time to think this over. Decide if you want to keep lying or if you want me around.'

She hissed. 'You're filth, Henry Lee Lucas. Worse than the dirt you walk on.'

'I'll bet you take that back too after you been missing me a couple days.' He gave her a glimpse of that old charming smile again. It didn't work, not even a little. 'Don't ever come back here. Not ever.'

The smile faded away to blankness. All emotion slipping out of his voice. 'Don't go ruining them girls' lives just to get one over on me.'

Betty shuddered. 'Get out, Henry! Get out!'

A road-trip with Henry was usually a fun time, and Wade had been looking forward to the run down to West Virginia. He was aghast to discover that his usually cheerful cousin had fallen into a dark mood.

It took a hundred miles before Wade's poking and prodding got Henry talking again, but once the flood gates were opened there was no shutting him up. 'Betty's trying to get rid of me. She's gone against me. She's telling all sort of nasty lies. Going to go spreading them lies around. Ruin my life. Evil bitch.'

No matter how Wade tried to change the subject, Henry just wouldn't stop. 'I can't go back there, cuz. I can't go back. Betty'll ruin everything if I do. Spread her filthy lies around. Make me look like a monster. I can't do it.'

This went on and on until they rolled to a halt in the traffic. A bridge was under repair up ahead, narrowing the road to just a single lane and causing the backup. Henry cranked down his window, still mumbling to himself about Betty.

'You talking to me, buddy?' There was a lorry parked alongside them, waiting for the chance to cross the bridge, a big freight hauler with the driver hanging half out the window.

'Just jawing to myself, mister.'

The trucker chuckled. 'Well, that's one way to make sure you don't get no surprises.'

Henry smiled up at him without even meaning to. He just looked at him for a while, then he finally asked. 'Where are you headed?'

There was a white-toothed grin under the trucker's moustache. 'I'm on my way to Shreveport, Louisiana. How about you?'

Henry glanced across at Wade, contemplated his options, and said, 'Well, I guess I'm heading to Shreveport, too, if you'll give me a ride?'

The trucker chuckled. 'Hell, I ain't got no company. Come on up here then.'

Just like that, Henry's brief attempt at normalcy fell to pieces all over again. He vanished from official records and began to drift. In Shreveport, his new friend gave him a stolen car to drive to Los Angeles, but it never quite made it there. Even in criminal circles, Henry became a ghost.

A Match Made in Hell

For a while, Henry Lee Lucas was nothing but a story. The one-eyed drifter of campfire tales. He travelled far and wide, with sightings of him now recorded in Wilmington, Delaware, and Hurst, Texas. He stopped for a while with Opal, who had forgiven him pretty readily for bringing murder to her doorstep when it came with the opportunity to be free of her mother forever, but stories gradually made their way through the family grapevine back to Opal.

He had been staying for a month with their other sister, Almeda, when she discovered that he was molesting her granddaughter, and sent him packing with the local sheriff on his heels. Opal had children of her own now, and as much as she might have cared for her goofy little brother, she wasn't blind nor stupid enough to let the same sort of situation develop there in Michigan.

All the doors that used to be open to him slammed shut as stories of his depravity managed to outpace him. His last real contact with his family was another visit to Almeda. She greeted him with a shotgun, but he insisted he wasn't there to see his grand-niece, nor even Almeda. He was there about scrapping work for her husband, who owned the local yard. While he was at the yard, he stole a partially refurbished truck and the wrecker's tags that would allow him to drive around in it without leaving an official record.

The next sign of Henry Lee Lucas's existence was towards the end of 1977 when he popped up very briefly in Beckley, West Virginia. Following some sort of injury, he found himself briefly hospitalised, and then unable to drift for a few months. So Henry did what he always had, found himself a simple woman to prey upon, and found the kind of job where a man of substantial strength could make some cash with no need for papers being filed. The woman in this case was a local legend named Rhonda Knuckles.

They say that men are attracted to women who remind them of their mother. And when presented with evidence like Rhonda Knuckles, it is hard to dispute that idea. She had more children than could be easily counted with more fathers than could be easily named—a veritable smorgasbord for a child predator like Henry Lee Lucas.

He found work in the local carpet warehouse, hauling product around and measuring it out for cutting and distribution, and he lingered for just a little while longer than he had intended to. Allegations of child molestation, not only from the Knuckles brood, but also from other children around town started up, and it was mentioned to Henry by his supervisor that the folks in these parts weren't overly attached to the letter of the law. There was an old lynching tree not far out of town that hadn't seen any use in some years, but it still looked sturdy enough to hold one body at least.

Henry left town the next morning in a borrowed pick-up truck, heading south and east to the one corner of the American South that hadn't yet served as his home.

By the spring of 1978, he had arrived in Florida. Flat broke and with no leads for work, he found himself standing in line at a soup kitchen in Jacksonville, Florida, which was where he bumped into the man who would become the centre of his world for the rest of his days.

The soft boy that Ottis had been was left long behind him. He bore the stubble and scars of a man now, looming over everyone around him at 6 feet, 8 inches. Henry fell into step with the lisping giant, fascinated by the juxtaposition of a clearly dangerous man and such effeminate mannerisms. Henry was no stranger to sex with men, but in prison and on the rough fringes of society where he'd dwelled, it had always been something secret, something shameful. Ottis had made homosexuality into a part of his personality, part of his identity. He had taken the thing that others would have used to shame him and worn it like armour. Henry could hardly take his eyes off the man.

To begin with, Ottis just took him for another closeted admirer, but after laying down a few hints that he would be amenable to spending some private time together, he was surprised to find that Henry genuinely seemed to want to be his friend. Neither man had ever had much luck or experience with friendship. Henry was too introverted and secretive to share much about himself, so those early days were spent trailing after Ottis as he went about his usual routine, rather than trying to seize control of the situation like he normally did.

There were two very specific moments in that first week that cemented the trust between the two men. The first was when Henry came with Ottis to visit his mother. She had died only two years previously, and every time that Ottis passed through Jacksonville he made sure to stop at her grave and pay his respects.

While Henry stood there, Ottis sank down onto the bare dirt and let out a sigh. 'It feels warm, you know? And if I just lay here for long enough, sometimes I can feel her moving underneath me. Like she's trying to give me a hug.'

The fact that both of them were haunted by their own mothers' ghosts was enough to convince Henry that the connection between them ran deeper. But he was still reticent to share any details of his own life, even though Ottis had now picked up on the underlying mystery of his new admirer and started prying at it. As evening rolled around, he asked Henry if he'd like to go for a drink, and ever his father's son, Henry most certainly did.

They made one brief stop at Ottis's car before they headed out for the night so that he could change. It was almost like a test, to see how far Henry could be pushed. A test that he passed with flying colours, both by openly admiring the other man's bare body as he stripped out of his dirty clothes and by voicing no objection when Ottis pulled on a sequinned dress.

In the first bar, they got a lot of dirty looks, and more than a few laughs, but nobody was deep enough in their drink to cause any trouble yet. Even in the second bar, Ottis was a source of amusement rather than anger. Henry found himself bobbing along in the other man's wake, enjoying his company and his sharp-tongued comments. It was only after the second bar, as they were heading towards the third, that the trouble started. Some local meathead hurled a mouthful of abuse at Ottis. The word 'abomination' came up. It only had time to come up once before Ottis was on the man, fists swinging wildly. The local had friends, and before Henry knew what he was doing, he was in a fist-fight in the streets, defending the honour of a man in a dress whom he'd met only a couple of days before. They held their own against that first crowd, but then a second wave of locals came pouring out of the bar and came after them. Henry had to grab Ottis by the arm and bodily drag him off the man whom he was beating to a bloody pulp. 'Come on, now. Ain't no trouble worth dying over.'

For one wild moment it seemed like Ottis was going to turn his unbridled rage on Henry, too, but then his eyes seemed to focus. He leaned in and gave him a kiss on the cheek, then the two of them ran for their life back to Ottis's car. There was only one man from the crowd of their attackers stupid enough to chase them down. Only one man consumed enough by hate that just the sight of a man in a dress made him think that he could take the two of them on. He caught up to them in an alleyway just a street from where they'd been heading, screaming slurs at the top of his lungs as he rounded the corner. The sight that awaited him was enough to steal the scream from his throat. Ottis had reached into his purse and pulled out a revolver. With a grunt of carnal delight, he pulled the trigger. Not just once, but six times. Stalking closer as the man fell to ensure every bullet hit its mark.

He turned back to Henry, eyes hazy with lust, blood splattered across his dress. 'You alright with that, sugar?'

Henry smiled right back at him. 'Most definitely.'

The Grand Tour

Their first meeting in Florida precipitated a rapid exit. Both Henry and Ottis were more than accustomed to skipping town ahead of trouble, and this time was no different. Except that it was. They weren't running off alone, scattering to the winds—they were together. For the first time in their lives, Henry and Ottis had both found someone who could know the entirety of them and not flinch away in fear. It was a terribly empowering experience for both of them, to know that they were not alone in the universe, to know for the very first time that they were not the sole recipients of minds completely different from those of everyone around them. In the sweaty confines of Ottis's car, the two of them traded stories of their lives, punctuated by their murders.

Ottis had managed to avoid detection as a murderer up until this point simply because his drifting habits happened to coincide perfectly with the 'best practices' that Henry had learned from his time reading sealed records and crime reports. He would commit a few crimes here and there, still relying almost entirely on prostitution and petty larceny to support his low-cost lifestyle. But by the time the local police caught wind of him, he had already moved on. Once or twice he had been arrested and jailed for lesser crimes, but because none of the justice departments around the country communicated with one another, each time he was caught, it was treated as his first offence rather than a pattern of criminal behaviour. On top of that, his incredibly effete mannerisms really helped to curb any fear that a jury might have of this lumbering giant of a man. The same thing that made people think of him as a freak outside of the courtroom also conferred on him a layer of unexpected protection inside it.

Both men had developed a taste for killing by this point in their lives. Henry as a means to an end and Ottis as a source of unique moments of pleasure in an otherwise dull and grey world. Neither man shared the same perspective on murder, but it didn't take them long before they realised that the diversity in their viewpoints was actually to their advantage. Ottis killed because he loved to kill. Because it aroused him. Henry killed out of practicality for the most part, and to procure a sexual outlet when willing warm bodies were in short supply. There was no reason that the two of them could not co-exist perfectly, fulfilling both of their needs with each victim.

It did not take long before they tested that theory. On their way out of Florida, the duo realised that they were short on funds, so they staged a quick liquor store robbery in Alabama. Just before they walked in the door, Ottis tossed the gun to Henry with a grin. Their relationship was intense so far, but it was also new, and Ottis had no real way of knowing if all of the things that Henry was telling him were the truth. This was his way of getting to the truth fast. Either Henry was a killer, or he wasn't. If he was, then they were going to have a real good time. If he wasn't, then there was no reason to be scared of putting a pistol in his hands. Either way, Ottis would get all the benefits of a robbery with none of the potential backlash for swinging a gun around. He was smarter than he looked.

Henry did not disappoint his new friend, storming into the store with the gun already pointed at the clerk without even a moment's hesitation. 'Listen up, you. Give us all the cash or I'll splat you all over them cigarettes. Hell, give us some of them cigarettes, too. And a bottle of whiskey. Move it or lose it.'

The clerk panicked, eyes wild and darting back and forth between the two men. To Henry, he looked like he might just be about to do something crazy.

'Don't you try shit, boy.'

Panic overrode whatever logic was operating the clerk's body. He tried to make a run for the door to the back room. Ottis's revolver was almost deafening in this enclosed space. Each of the three shots roared out of it and echoed back at them. All three bullets hit the running clerk in the back. Square in the middle. Tidy as any firing range cut-out.

When his hearing came back, Henry was almost deafened all over again by Ottis's whooping. He found himself wrapped in a gangly armed hug and had a stubbly kiss pressed to his forehead. 'Oh, you did it, sugar. You did it just right.'

Ottis didn't even bother with the cash register; he went straight for the dead body and started to unbuckle the dead clerk's belt. Henry just stood there staring, mesmerised as Ottis got the boy's trousers down far enough to serve his purposes. After the gunfire and yelling, the store was almost deafeningly quiet. Henry could hear every panting breath coming out of Ottis. He moved over to the counter silently to collect the cash, but his eyes never left the scene by the back wall. Ottis let out a little moan, then glanced back, suddenly aware of the eyes on him. 'You can go wait in the car if you like. Or you can watch if that's what takes your fancy.' Henry leaned back against the counter and stared at Ottis, almost defiantly. 'Oh, so you're the watching kind, are you, sugar?'

It was another little challenge. Another little push to see just how far Henry would go. As it turned out, all the way. They had sex for the first time in the garbage-strewn back seat of Ottis's car just a few miles down the road from that murder. Both of them all worked up by the night's work. Henry didn't want to talk about it afterwards, and Ottis had already pushed him so far for one night that he didn't dare go any further. After all, he still had the gun, and now Ottis knew for certain that he was ready and willing to use it.

The two of them roamed the southern states for months on end. Aimlessly killing, raping, and robbing as they saw fit. Their sex life was inconsistent. If they found themselves in the middle of nowhere and Henry had no other outlet then he would happily take Ottis in the back seat of the car, but if there were women about, his preference was pretty clear. The times that Ottis interfered with Henry's flirting were among the only times the two of them disagreed at all.

Henry Lee Lucas and Ottis Toole working in tandem, was a thing of nightmares. For a year, they were on the road sharing the lessons that they had learned, screwing and arguing, and getting blind drunk by the roadside until all those things blended into one long, loud blur. Henry taught Ottis the things that he needed to do to circumvent the methods that the police might employ to catch him; how to mangle a body before burying it so that it couldn't be identified, how to strip the plates off a car and run it around with wrecker's tags so that it was always overlooked. In return, Ottis taught Henry new depths of depravity. Their sexual relationship didn't show Henry anything that he hadn't seen a dozen times before in prison showers, but their criminal relationship was something else entirely. Necrophilia was part and parcel of Henry's usual behaviour, but Ottis kept pushing him to go further. To have sex with the decomposing bodies of their victims when they had to wait out a day before the cover of darkness could cloak an improvised burial. To eat the flesh of the dead, grilled by the roadside on a tiny barbecue that Ottis hauled from one stolen car's boot to the next. Henry tasted it only once before declaring that he didn't like Ottis's barbecue sauce and never indulging in cannibalism again. It seemed strange that he was the one with more scruples for the first time in his life, but it grew stranger still when it became apparent how much he dominated the relationship. After their first night together, Henry no longer felt any need to prove himself to Ottis, and with the arrival of that fresh influx of confidence, the other man suddenly discovered an overwhelming attraction to Henry. Ottis made the most foolish mistake in a lifetime full of them: he fell in love with Henry.

There is no telling how many people they killed in that first year of travelling together, in no small part due to the number of confessions that the two men made, recanted, and then made all over again when it suited their purposes. When you piece together the details of their confessions and see where they overlap, it was clear that the presence of another killer drove each of them to new heights. They spent a surprising amount of time trying to top the other's latest activities.
One story that both men told in vivid detail was about the time that they spotted a young couple hitchhiking through Texas. Henry was driving that night, trying to settle his backside into the pristine seat of the freshly stolen car they had picked up only a few towns back. They had to put some distance between them and the vehicle's owner before it was reported to the local sheriff. That was why they planned on driving through the night, intent on burning through the whole tank of gas and a whole strip of the highway before anyone knew anything was amiss. The kids by the roadside were in their late teens, or maybe early twenties. The girl hung back behind her boy as if he could protect her from all the things that went bump in the night. They were perfect, both of them the very image of white picket fence America.
Henry nudged Ottis awake and pulled over. The boy held up a hand in greeting as the passenger side's door swung open. Ottis held up a gun in answer. He blew off half the boy's fingers with the first shot, then turned his aim towards his torso, rattling out the other five bullets so fast that the girl didn't even have a chance to scream. Henry was not sitting idle as his friend and lover went to work; he had sprung out of the car and rounded it

before the last shot was fired. The girl tried to run, but horror had turned her feet to lead. She stumbled and staggered as she turned towards the desert, and before she'd made it a step Henry was on her. His dirty hands tore at her clothes. His stale beer breath swept hot over her face as he pawed at her. She managed to clench a fist and swing at Henry's face, but it was like hitting a brick wall. His grin didn't falter. He didn't even seem to notice. He just wrapped his arms around her waist and lifted her clean off the packed sand. There was one awful dizzy moment when gravity let go of her, alongside all other logic and reason, but then she was orientated to the earth once more, slung over this monstrous man's shoulder with a clear view of everything he had trod on, and the empty stretch of nothing that was all she could see in any direction. She screamed anyway, not out of any hope of being heard, but as the only outlet for the absolute terror that filled her. All that did was make him laugh.

She could see everything that was happening behind her. She could see what the other man, the huge lumbering monster, was doing to her dead boyfriend. She could hear every grunt and every groan even when she pressed her eyes shut against it. Henry patted her on the backside as she went limp, and she had a terrible premonition of her future. She cracked the back of her head on the frame of the car door as he tossed her into the backseat, filling her head up with ringing darkness. As he climbed on top of her, she tried to chase that darkness down into the safety of unconsciousness, but her body betrayed her. It brought her back up to feel his callous fingers dragging over her bare skin, his browned teeth nipping at her stomach.

Ottis got back in the car while Henry was still raping the girl in the backseat, more than satisfied with his own evening's entertainment. He preferred his men hot to cooling, but he wasn't fussy, and killing a man came with its own special zing. It sounded like Henry was still going to take a while, though, and they had places to go, so he started up the car and they took off down the highway, screams trailing out behind them.

Neither man was a stranger to the road, but while Henry was just learning all the ways that belonging to nowhere made him free, Ottis was different. He had a longing to live amongst other people, even if they hated him. He was hopelessly lovesick over Henry, but their constant isolation and proximity was making the sweetness of that love turn bitter. He wanted Henry to love him back, but the other man didn't seem capable. Whether that was because Ottis was a man, or whether it was because of the echoing void in Henry where other people would keep their emotions, didn't much matter. Ottis could already sense how easily his love could transform into resentment and hatred if things went on as they had, and he had no desire to turn Henry into an enemy. If they settled somewhere then other people could serve as a buffer, an inoculation of social interaction to make it seem like Henry wasn't the only other person in the world.

For Ottis, home meant Florida. He hadn't stopped by his mother's grave for a whole year, the longest he'd ever stayed away, and while he loathed his family, he still felt their absence keenly. Henry didn't want to go. He didn't want to settle anywhere. He dug his heels into the ground and railed against it. Then they drove down to Florida.

The intense relationship that he'd cultivated with Ottis was a double-edged sword. He knew every soft spot in the other man's psyche, but he had left himself just as exposed and open to manipulation. Ultimately, neither of them was ready for the ride to end just yet, and they were both willing to make some compromises to stay together.

The Child Bride

Ottis's family did not know how to respond to Henry. They didn't know if Ottis was bringing home a friend, a lover, or something in between. The way that the men behaved together gave very little away, and while Ottis was so flamboyant that his sexuality was often apparent to people several streets over, Henry was a closed book. They drifted around the periphery of the Toole family, never quite welcomed in, and never quite rejected fully. The duo stayed with several of Ottis's sisters during their first few months in Jacksonville, bouncing from one apartment to the next as their presence became a nuisance. Ottis's sisters had been a font of constant misery to him in his earlier life, but now, with their mother and her constant incitements to torment him gone, they had all fallen into more traditional familial relationships. Henry swiftly found himself occupying exactly the same role as Ottis in those households, an honorary uncle to all of Ottis's nephews and nieces, including Frank and Freida, the twin children of his eldest sister, Drucilla.

Drucilla was a single parent working well past the limits of her own endurance to try to support her family, and she was incredibly relieved to find a pair of ready-made babysitters snoozing on her living room furniture at all hours of the day. She might have found something suspicious about the way that this near-stranger Henry took an interest in her children. If he favoured one or the other, he made a point of lavishing attention on both of them equally, even taking them with him and Ottis when they went on short road trips around Florida.

Henry honestly didn't care for Frank much—he considered the boy to be a whimpering simpleton for the most part—but he endured his company in exchange for the access that it granted him to Frank's sister. At ten years old, Frieda was the apple of Henry's eye, and he took a more than paternal interest in her, just as he had in the children of his ex-wife.

Almost immediately after meeting her he started calling her 'Becky' in private. Neither of them cared for her given name, and she thrilled every time she heard him whispering the one that he had given her. Henry had read the records of many child abducting paedophiles in his time—he knew just how easily they got caught out when taking their pliant victims in public just because they slipped up and called them by their real name. He was training both himself and Frieda for that possibility. To this day, nobody is entirely clear on what it was about Frieda Powell that was so incredibly appealing to Henry Lee Lucas, whether it was her close connection to the uncle that Henry was unwilling to admit that he loved, or if there were something in her pubescent personality that meshed perfectly with his own networked web of psychoses. Whatever the attachment was, both of them called it love, and when the time came to be moving on, Henry dug in his heels all over again.

He wasn't ready to give up on the road entirely. Even through the months when they had been staying in Jacksonville, the duo often took extended trips out on the highways and byways, preying on any pedestrians they found outside of civilisation and committing armed robberies where they dared—but Henry wasn't ready to break off his tenuous relationship with Frieda, either. It wasn't clear if he had begun sexually abusing her by this point, although later arguments that the duo would have in earshot of witnesses would seem to indicate some degree of chastity on Henry's part for possibly the first time in his life.

Ottis took a wife in 1979, a train-wreck of a relationship that saw him publicly outed as gay to everyone in Jacksonville by her fierce rumour spreading after the whole relationship fell apart. She never named the lover that he had brought home and kicked her out of her own bedroom to have sex with, but to everyone who knew Ottis, it was abundantly clear that the lover was Henry. It created an extremely uncomfortable situation for Ottis, who would normally have skipped town after creating such a fuss, and he had many hissed arguments with Henry to that effect.

To stay close to Frieda, Henry, and by proxy Ottis, had to get jobs in town. Southeast Color Coat was a roofing company in Jacksonville that Henry somehow managed to impress with his technical skills, and by the end of his interview both men were on the company payroll, although their wages were often docked for failure to show up to work—the call of the highway and the life of crime that they both adored was just too loud to ignore some days.

According to their confessions, this was the most fruitful time in Henry and Ottis's careers as murderers, and while the thousands of murders that they confessed to could not possibly have all happened, there is one murder that definitely did.

In Georgetown, Texas, a hitchhiker from Oklahoma died. Her body was found dumped by the side of the road, stripped completely naked with the exception of a pair of orange socks. To this day, she has not been identified, although there was so much publicity around the case that her lack of identification is likely the most miraculous thing about her death at this point. She died by strangulation at the side of Interstate 35 and was tossed over a barrier to fall into the dirt, where she would later be discovered. These are the certain facts of the 'Orange Socks' murder. Beyond that, everything is shrouded in lies by either one serial killer or the other.

According to Henry, he picked up the girl when he was travelling alone, and they had consensual sex by the roadside. When she refused to have sex with him for a second time, saying 'not right now,' he had swerved the car to the side of the road and strangled her to death while raping her.

According to Ottis, she was a regular lover of Henry's whom he had murdered in a fit of jealousy at seeing his lover in the arms of another. Initially, Ottis claimed to have slit her throat while the two of them were having sex, but upon hearing about the forensic evidence, he altered his story to include garrotting with a pair of stockings. Regardless of which story was the truth, the duo were able to provide some very specific details, both about the location of the body and some material evidence found around the corpse that only someone who was present at the scene of the crime could have known—details that were not even included in the police reports because they were considered to be irrelevant, like a folded hand towel that 'Orange Socks' had been using in lieu of a sanitary napkin.

Despite their near-constant absences from work, Henry and Ottis managed to keep their heads down well enough to hold onto those jobs for two whole years. Years in which Henry had more time to ingratiate himself with the ever-flattered Frieda. Henry and Ottis maintained that holding pattern, working, robbing, killing, and raping as they needed to throughout all of that time, just waiting for the catalyst that would remake their lives all over again. It arrived in 1981, when Ottis's sister, and the twins' mother, hung herself in their apartment. The children were the ones to find her.

Henry and Ottis immediately swept in to lay claim to the children, now twelve years old, over the widespread protests of the extended Toole family. The other sisters were in no better position to care for the children than Ottis, and the kids barely knew most of them by this point, having spent almost two years in Henry's loving care.

From that moment on, both children rode in the back of the pickup truck everywhere that Henry and Ottis went, sitting outside their roofing jobs in the sweltering heat and parked outside the petrol stations in the cool of the night while their ersatz parents went in to rob and murder. There are few secrets in so confined a space, and there are even fewer that can't be seen with just a glance through the bug-crusted windshield. Both children understood exactly what their new guardians were doing, but they responded to that information in completely different ways.

'Becky' had already fallen deeply for Henry, in the way that only extremely naive young girls can. His perfection had become a cornerstone of her worldview, and anything that might disrupt that idealisation would have hurt her, so her rejection of such, along with the law, was a guiding force in her life. If Henry broke the law, it was because the law was wrong. If he killed people, then they needed killing.

Frank went mad. Whether this was a symptom of the mental weakness that Henry had always ascribed to him or the inevitable result of so much disruption in his young life is unclear. His whole life fell apart with the death of his mother, and the people who were meant to take care of him turned out to be hardened criminals with very little interest in his mental state most of the time or even an interest in his survival. In a fictional retelling of these events, he would have witnessed one of Henry and Ottis's gruesome murders, and his mind would have broken. But in reality, it was just the slow grind of life in their care that drove him into the near catatonic state he was in by the time the slow gears of child protective services finally started turning.

Both children were taken from school to juvenile homes where they would remain in the care of the state until they turned eighteen. From there, Frank was soon transferred to a hospital for the mentally infirm, where he remained for the rest of his short life.

In the home, they called her Frieda, and it felt like a lie each and every time she answered to it. She wasn't Frieda anymore, she was Becky, his Becky. The other girls in the house picked on her for her name or for being dirty, or for whatever fresh excuse they had conjured up that day, but all of their little barbs passed her by.

She didn't belong here. She belonged out there on the road with the man she loved. Every night she would press her face to the window pane and stare out into the clammy darkness beyond the bars. From up in this room she could see the road beyond the high wall and its mask of trees. She had been staring out intently ever since she first arrived, certain in her gut that this wasn't the end for her, positive that her love would never abandon her. She stared out at that road as if she could will a shabby looking pickup truck into existence. She imagined it so intently that when she finally set eyes on the car idling out there she was almost certain that it was all just a dream. From here she couldn't be certain, she didn't know that it was Henry who got out of the passenger's side and slunk over to the wall, but she had been waiting for this too long to care.

Sneaking downstairs wasn't hard—there was a steady flow of movement throughout the house as they all went to the communal bathrooms at odd hours, but the front door was going to be hard to get around. They locked it at sundown. She needn't have worried. By the time she made it down, Henry was already there, crowbar in hand and a grin plastered over his face. If they were smart they would have run. But they were romantics, so he scooped her up in his arms and kissed her like a hero in a movie.

At the wall, he boosted her up, and for the first time all night, anxiety slithered through her. It was a high wall. How was she going to get down on the other side? 'Just drop, sugar, I'll catch you.'

Ottis was there, smiling just as wide as Henry had been. She fell into his arms with a little yip, and her uncle gave her one last squeeze for good measure, so that she knew that she was safe, so that she could know for certain that she was home again.

They went on lingering around Jacksonville for almost a full year after breaking Becky out of juvenile detention, but by January of 1982 the authorities were closing in on them. Their crimes had gone almost entirely undetected up until this point thanks to the invaluable education that Henry had received in Ionia State. But Becky could not avoid attention. There was an official record of her escape from care and there was an active effort to return her to state custody. Confronted with the choice of staying in Florida and being separated from Henry, or fleeing across the country with the two men, there wasn't any choice to be made at all.

This time, when Ottis and Henry set off drifting across the southern states, it was with a girl in the backseat of the car. She was the perfect addition to their little family unit; willing to overlook the two of them rutting in the dirt by the side of the car when they thought she was asleep, willing to turn her gaze away when they robbed and butchered with abandon, and serving all the time as the perfect camouflage. The two men alone were frightening, even with Ottis's flamboyance. But with the addition of a girl that the two of them looked on with obvious love and care, they were able to slip right under the radar of anyone on the lookout for danger. Victims came willingly into their reach. Suspicion passed them by entirely. Everything was easier when there were three of them. While they were together, it was the happiest time in their lives. But even for serial killers, all good things have to come to an end.

Abandonment Issues

Less than three months into their journey together, Ottis took ill. He had been a devoted alcoholic since he was old enough to open a bottle on his own, and with time the liquor had eaten away at his liver, causing all manner of minor medical problems. This time, he took on a jaundiced appearance, grew sluggish, and vomited each time he tried to ingest food. Neither Henry nor Becky had a clue what to do to help him. They turned around and headed back to Florida, delivering him to the first hospital that they found, then turned tail and fled before the authorities could notice Becky's presence. Ottis had never been so thoroughly abandoned before. His family had always been toxic, but they had been persistent. They may have hated him, but they would never ever have let him go.

It took almost a month more before he had recovered enough from his illness to get out of the hospital, and by then he had no way of tracking his lover and niece down. He was stranded, angry, and trained to kill without detection by one of the best minds in the serial killing hobby. It didn't take him long before he found an outlet for his frustrations.

At first, he fell back into old patterns, setting fires for the rush of arousal that accompanied each act of arson, but after experiencing the intensity of murder on a regular basis he found that arson had lost its thrill; at least until he started setting fire to buildings in Jacksonville that he knew had people sleeping inside. Two people died as a result of the fires that he had started, and while that aroused him greatly, it also drew unwanted attention. He stole himself a white Cadillac and went for a drive all the way down the east coast. It was there, in Hollywood, Florida, that Ottis would have his next brush with celebrity.

Adam Walsh didn't want to go to the shop. He was six years old and department stores had very little appeal to him, particularly on balmy days at the end of July when there was baseball to play. The mall was kind of cool, he supposed. The air conditioning was kind of nice after a long, sticky few months. The mall even had toy stores and stuff that he'd really rather go visit than Sears, but his mother had her heart set on some lamp that was on sale, so he went along quietly, the way he went along quietly with just about everything in life. He didn't like to be the centre of attention, and he didn't like it when there was trouble. If he could keep his head down and keep his mother smiling, then that was exactly what he would do, especially if it meant they might go by the toy store on the way out of the mall.

Sears was just as boring as ever. Adam could feel the boredom settling over him like a heavy blanket. Even his mother, lost in conversation with the first salesperson she could lay hands on, noticed him slump. That was when something caught her eye and a little smile lit up her face. She dragged his unwilling body over to a small crowd of other boys a little bit older than him, over by the boring microwaves and stuff. There was bleeping and music coming from in the middle of the press of jostling bodies, like at the arcade. The weight of boredom lessened slightly as she pressed him in close enough to see the display. An Atari! The other boys were taking turns playing the games. Adam wanted a shot so badly, but he could see that there was already a kind of queue, one that was already kind of shaky without him wedging himself in. Mother had already vanished out of sight by the time he thought to look back. That was fine. This was way more interesting than some stupid lamp.

The other boys were getting excited. They were shouting, and if Adam had a little more courage he might have been shouting with them, but instead, he just lurked at the back of the pack, ducking and bobbing to see the screen through them all. One game ended and another began, but there was some confusion over who had the next turn. One of the boys was still holding tight to his controller and another two were trying to snatch the other out of each other's grasp. It escalated to pushing and yet more shouting before the long shadow of a security guard loomed over them. 'All right, that is enough. Out you go.'

He held out his arms and herded them along, and Adam was herded along with them. The other boys were bigger, ten or twelve; they were probably here on their own. But Adam had to get back before Mother found him missing. He kept trying to say something, to find his voice through the shyness, but it just didn't come. Before he knew it, he was outside, not just back in the mall but out on the street, and the guard had lumbered back inside. He turned to talk to the other boys, but they were already striding off down the street together, laughing and jostling each other like nothing had even happened. Adam didn't know where to go. He didn't know what to do. He'd heard about 'getting lost' but he'd never once thought that it could happen to him. He was a good boy who always did what he was told, so no bad things could happen to him, right? There were adults passing by him in the street, but none of them even looked down. If he went back into the shop, would the security guard still be waiting for him? Would he get in even bigger trouble? His mother would not be happy with him. She would be mad, like the time he went out into the garden to play without telling her first. Complex decision making was not part of the six-year-old skill-set, so when he heard a soft voice cooing to him from the roadside, it was a relief more than anything else. Even if going over to the car was the wrong decision, at least someone else was making it for him. 'You all right there, sugar? Where's your momma?'

There was a big white Cadillac sitting there by the side of the road, like something out of a movie, and that voice, it sounded like something out of a movie, too. Like some Disney character had come to life. 'Are you lost, little boy? You want to come with me? I've got a ton of toys to play with in here. Got some candy, too, if you're hungry.'

It was a ploy right out of some after-school special, but Adam was too young to have even the beginnings of a fear of strangers instilled in him. He walked up to the car slowly, out of shyness rather than fear. Inside, Ottis was waiting for him. 'You ever get to ride up front when you're out with your folks?'

'N-no.'

'You want to give it a try? Have a roll round the block and look for your momma?'

Adam nodded and reached for the handle. It was a better plan than the nothing he'd been able to come up with. Inside the car, it smelt kind of funny, like his clothes after he'd been playing baseball all day in the sunshine, but he didn't say anything to the nice man. That would be rude. The nice man looked a little bit funny, too. He was really big, and his stringy hair was getting kind of thin on the top like he was smuggling a big egg underneath it. But he was smiling down at Adam really friendly, so he decided not to worry about it. They drove along the street and turned to the left, just like the man said they would. Adam pressed his nose to the glass and stared out at the crowds, but there was no sign of his mother anywhere. She was probably still arguing about her stupid lamp with some salesperson in Sears.

'You know, I've been thinking, I'd like a little boy like you for myself. My buddy, Henry. He got himself a little girl. My niece. And if he has that, why can't I?'

Adam turned slowly in the seat to look at the man, confused and still too shy to say much of anything. Ottis didn't falter. 'I mean, sure, you're kind of little compared to her. Folks ain't going to mistake you for my wife or nothing. But you and me, we could work out just fine. You could be my son. Not ever going to have none any other way. And I'd take good care of you, and you could love me like a boy is supposed to. How does that sound to you, son?'

Adam was more confused than afraid. What was the man talking about? They carried on straight ahead instead of turning left at the next junction, and that was enough to finally force words out of him. 'I need to go back.'

'Ain't no need for going back, sugar. You're with me now. You'll keep me company. You'll love me. You'll do anything I ask you to, just like folks that love you are meant to.'

Adam was scared now. Actually scared instead of the make-believe scared he was in his games. He wanted his mother. 'I want my mom.'

Ottis chuckled like the kid was just being silly. 'I'm your mom now, sugar. I'll feed you and clothe you and...'

'I want my mom!' Adam insisted, finally finding his voice.

Ottis's fist lashed out, nearly as big as Adam's whole face. Adam didn't feel the punch. One minute there was a sense of motion then the whole world just went white. The pain crept in a moment later and tears started streaming down his reddened face. 'Let me out! I want my mom!'

Ottis's face was frozen in a rictus of frustration. A quick smack was meant to quiet the kid down, not rile him up even more. 'No. No!'

Adam scrabbled at the lock on the car, trying to fling himself out on the side of the highway, but Ottis was having none of it. He hammered the little boy in the head with his meaty fist, over and over. Screaming to drown out the sounds of the little boy's sobbing. Then, it was finally quiet.

Ottis drove until the sun was slipping behind the mangrove trees, then he pulled off the dirt track he'd been following to deal with Adam more permanently. When he reached in to drag the boy out, he couldn't believe that the kid was still breathing. Still grumbling at being woken from his concussed slumber. All of the rage and bitter disappointment that Ottis was feeling after Henry abandoned him came bubbling up. He wrapped his fingers around little Adam's tiny throat and he squeezed as tightly as he could until he could feel the bones. Then he let the tiny corpse drop to the dirt, and his training from all those years with Henry kicked in.

He fetched a machete out of the trunk and with three brutal cuts took the boy's head clean off. The rest of the body he would take back to somewhere more familiar and burn away to bones and ash, but the head made it too easy to identify. Dental records were the thing Henry kept banging on about. Easiest just to dump the whole head somewhere it would never be found. Ottis tossed Adam's into a little canal near where he'd stopped and went back to clean up his mess. Whatever satisfaction he'd been hoping for was nowhere in sight.

The abduction of Adam Walsh became one of the most widely publicised crimes in American history, resulting in the passing of multiple laws for the protection of children, the creation of 'America's Most Wanted,' which was hosted by Adam's father for its duration, and a manhunt that would not end until 2008, when the police finally confirmed Ottis Toole's involvement. Prior to that confirmation, there was a great deal of speculation about who had killed young Adam, after his head was recovered from a drainage ditch early in the search for him, on the same day that a $10,000 reward was offered for his safe return. Interestingly enough, it would seem that Ottis Toole was not the only serial killer at the Hollywood Mall that day.

Jeffrey Dahmer lived in Florida at the time of Adam's abduction, and a man fitting his description was seen several times around the mall that day, including in the toy section of the Sears in question. Years later, the police confronted Dahmer with this evidence and demanded his confession, and he laughed in their faces. He was imprisoned on multiple life sentences with no possibility of parole, and he had quite happily confessed to every one of his crimes once he had been caught. He pointed out the flaw in the police's logic. If he had committed the crime, he had nothing to lose and everything to gain by admitting it, so when he denied it, they could believe him.

Ottis returned to Jacksonville the following day, found an abandoned refrigerator, and used it as a makeshift incinerator for the rest of Adam's remains—the same solution that Henry had been using to dispose of their victims for many years when circumstances allowed. He started a few more fires, started a few bar fights, and let the days and weeks pass him by in a grey haze of misery. He would never find love again, and he had no way to chase it. All that he could do was wait, and hope.

Without Ottis to drive them on, Henry decided to try and create some sort of settled life for him and Becky. She had grown enough now that the prospect of them being a couple wasn't so ridiculous to the outside observer, so they took on a rented apartment in Maryland under the pretence of being newlyweds. Henry found himself work at the local scrapyard, and they began to settle into the sort of routine that in anyone else's life might be considered normal, but that for both Henry and Becky was now a bizarre deviation from their usual behaviour. Play-acting, at normalcy.

Becky was completely isolated from everyone around her. She dare not get to know the neighbours in case details of her life came slipping out, and while Henry was free to come and go as he pleased, staying out until the middle of the night sometimes, she soon discovered that there was an invisible tether holding her in easy walking distance of their tiny flea-ridden apartment. With no other outlet, her feelings for Henry intensified. He became her whole world. She was nearing fifteen years old, and all of the idealised romance that had defined their relationship thus far was now confronted with the hormonal reality of a developing teenager. Henry was her husband, in every way except for the ones that mattered, and she wanted to change that. She knew that he was having sex with other women when he was out on those late nights. She knew that he had needs that weren't being fulfilled by their relationship, and it made her furious. She was his wife, and she wanted him to be her husband in every way. Including in the bedroom.

The first time that she tried to mount him while they were kissing, he nearly flung her across the room. The next time, he sat her down and gave his best rendition of a talk about the birds and the bees, along with several heavy-handed comments about her still being a little girl; comments that really did not go down well.

Sex became a major source of tension within their household, with Becky trying to pressure Henry into taking their relationship to the next level while he tried to resist the temptation—something that he had never been particularly successful at. The more that she pushed him, the more that he avoided her, and the more certain she was that he was out every night having sex with other women, driven wild with lust by her clumsy, fumbling attempts at seduction.

The unfortunate truth of the matter was that Henry was going out to satiate his sexual appetite in exactly the same way as he always had: through rape, murder, necrophilia, and sexual assault. His ability to intimidate and manipulate his victims had only improved over time, and all of the amateur mistakes that he had made in his early criminal career had served as useful lessons to him. He managed to last for months without a single whisper of his crimes making it to the police, despite being in a small town with a healthy gossip network. Then, one of the local girls, a teenager only slightly younger than Becky, came forward with her story about him forcing her hands down his trousers.

Henry was arrested for the sexual assault, and Becky was caught idling in their apartment. For a 'first offence,' he received a relatively short sentence of only three months in the local jail, but Becky's fate was considerably more permanent. She was easily matched to the missing persons records from Florida and shipped back there immediately, returned to the last relative that had official guardianship of her, with the intention that her family would put her on the path back to salvation. Ottis met her at the police station in Jacksonville with a grin on his face. Becky was back, and Henry would surely follow.

With his sentence served, Henry caught a ride on a freight train heading the right direction and made the whole journey without stopping for a rest. When he showed up on Ottis's doorstep, Becky and the lumbering giant swept him into a crushing hug. They were all right back where they belonged. The party that followed lasted almost a whole week, with all three of them drunk and dazed, but by the end of that week, every one of them was twitching to get out of Jacksonville again. They loaded into yet another 'borrowed' car and headed for California.

For Henry, this was the ideal situation. He got to have the relationship that he wanted with Becky, spend the time he enjoyed with Ottis, and had the other man there to serve as a buffer whenever she started to push for a sexual relationship. For the other two, it was less ideal. Becky wanted Henry all to herself, and her mounting jealousy started to drive a wedge between her and her uncle. For Ottis, it was like his worst nightmare come to life; seeing Henry every day, watching as his ever-developing relationship with Becky took him further and further out of his reach.

They stayed with friends and acquaintances, bouncing from one place to the next. In Hemet, California, they squatted in the home of Jack and O'Bere Smart, spending almost four months restoring furniture to earn their keep. The Smarts wanted rid of them after just one month, but the trio gave no real cause to put them out. They were loud and their love triangle was a little nauseating once the Smarts understood it. But beyond that, they did good work on the furniture and they kept mostly to themselves in the manner of people who have too much to hide. Eventually, O'Bere hit upon a solution. Her elderly mother had been haranguing her for years to come and care for her in Texas, and now they had a full set of handymen and housekeepers willing to work for room and board. Kate Rich was eighty years old, the proud matriarch of her family now fallen on hard times. Money wasn't a problem, but maintenance required people to be physically present, and with her kids dispersed across the states, that was something Kate was sorely lacking.

On the road to Texas, things finally reached a boiling point when Becky caught Henry and Ottis having sex while she was sleeping. She issued the first of her many ultimatums. Henry had to choose, there and then, which one of the Tooles he wanted to keep in his life. He could have Becky as his wife, body, and soul, or he could hold on to whatever sordid little relationship he had been sneaking about with Ottis to maintain. He was given until they reached Texas as a deadline to make his decision. Henry was not a man inclined towards introspection. Decisions in his life up until this point had served one of two purposes: survival and feeding his lusts. This was likely the most strenuous mental activity he had ever undertaken, and he hated every minute of it. All three of them travelled in sullen silence, their usual jokes and chatter muted by the impending dissolution that awaited them.

Ottis was miserable. There was no doubt in his mind whom Henry was going to choose, and he had spent the entire time that they were in each other's company avoiding this very conflict. He knew Henry preferred women. He knew that Henry was never going to love him the way that he wanted to be loved, but he had been able to hold out hope for as long as Henry kept him trailing along behind him. When they got to Texas, Ottis didn't even attempt to sway Henry in his favour; instead, he did his dearest friend one last kindness by taking the difficult decision out of his hands. Both Henry and Becky were dumped at the roadside, and Ottis drove off with tears in his eyes. It was the last time that the men would ever see each other.

Alone at Last

So it was, that Henry Lee Lucas and the girl known as Becky found themselves stranded on the side of the highway with a hundred miles of Texas between them and the closest shelter. Henry had been so lost in his first intellectual exercise that he had forgotten all about his own survival and comfort. He was not happy with Becky. She had taken his ideal life and ripped it to pieces in the name of her dream, and a more introspective duo might have realised that he was never going to be able to forgive that. As it was, they trudged together, weary and sun-beaten along the side of the road with their scant luggage and their thumbs held up hopefully towards every passing car. Time stretched out slow and lazy in the heat. Every minute could have been an hour. The midday sun beat down on them like they had done it some personal insult, and before long, Becky's litany of complaints started to tumble out of her. She was too hot. She was tired. Her feet hurt. Henry's hands clenched themselves into fists at the sound of her voice. He could have killed her there and then for what she had done to him, but then he would have been left with nothing at all. She was all that he had left in the world and letting go of that was too hard, even when the sound of her whining voice set his teeth on edge.

When a car finally stopped for them, Henry didn't even realise it at first. He was so beaten down. It was only when the driver stood up and loudly declared, 'Well, my children, you look like you have been through the wars,' that Henry finally snapped out of it.

'Hey, mister, any chance of a ride?' He didn't have the energy to muster a spiel.

Luckily, this was one stranger who didn't need reeling in. A stranger with his very own set of ulterior motives. 'Why of course! I didn't pull up here in the middle of nowhere for the good of my health. Whereabouts are you headed to?'

'We ain't fussy.' Becky groaned. 'Anywhere with some shade.'

The man grinned at her. 'Well, hop right in then, lovebirds! Let's get this show on the road!'

The car was cramped but clean, and with all the windows rolled down there was enough of a breeze to make it a vast improvement over standing out in the sun. The radio wasn't working, but the driver more than made up for that, filling every empty moment with more words. 'So, tell me, dear children. Would I be right in thinking that if you do not have a particular destination in mind, that might mean that you also have no place to hang your hat and call your own? That you are itinerants?'

Henry cocked his head. 'I don't know about that, mister, but we ain't got no place to be running back to if that's what you're asking?'

'Lost and in need of a shepherd, just as I suspected when I first set my eyes upon you. Allow me to introduce myself properly. I am the Reverend Ruben Moore, father, and preacher to the House of Prayer. We have ourselves a little place out here along this road. A little home for those without one. A place that you might call your own, were you so inclined.'

Henry chuckled. 'So you're just offering us a place to stay? No strings attached?'

It was like Moore already had the whole patter memorised. 'The only bondage I would set upon you would be the ties of friendship and community, my child. You would be free to come and go as you please, though I'd rather you didn't bring any sin or temptation down among the more vulnerable of our numbers. Newlyweds like you, you need the best start in life that the world can give you. I'm just doing as the Lord would want. Offering up what I've got and don't need to them that need but don't got.'

Henry was still dubious, but one glance back at Becky, all wide-eyed and excitable, told him exactly what she wanted. She loved to do the newlywed bit, and if they were living on some Jesus commune, she'd get to play that part to her heart's content.

'Alright, Rev, we're listening.' Henry settled back into his seat with a sigh. 'Tell us all about it.'

By the end of the day, Henry and Becky were settled into the 'honeymoon suite' of the House of Prayer's commune on the outskirts of Stoneburg, Texas. It was ideally situated for Henry and Becky, just a short drive to the south from Ringgold, where they were meant to be caring for Kate Rich. They had met a few of the other drifters and homeless people that Moore had reeled in with his patter and promises of a better life. Most of them now worked for the Reverend in his main enterprise, running a joinery and roofing company. The commune was as much a company town as it was a religious organisation, and it was as much a homeless shelter as either of the other two.

Henry barely got the door closed before Becky was on him, and this time he did nothing to fight her off. He had tried to keep their relationship pure. He had tried to keep from hurting her. But right now he was angry and confused with only one familiar thing to grab hold of, and he was going to hold onto it for all that he was worth. He hurt her, just like he'd been scared of doing. She wouldn't let him stop even as she bled. At long last, all of her dreams had come true. At long last, she was his wife in every way that mattered.

The next day, they borrowed one of the trucks from the commune and headed off to work. Kate Rich took an immediate liking to Becky and was willing to overlook her sullen husband in exchange for this new daughter. To Henry's eyes, the work that Becky was putting in seemed a lot like pottering around the house rather than actually doing anything, while he was doing hard manual labour every single day they were on the Rich property. But it was a small price to pay to keep the old bird sweet while he milked her bank account for everything that it was worth. The extensive repairs and refurbishments to the big old house came with a lot of material costs, costs that Kate had to sign so many cheques for that she eventually just started signing a few at a time and handing them off to Henry to finish with the details. This wasn't his usual kind of crime, but he'd done enough reading on the subject to know how people usually got caught out. When he started making out cheques for himself, he kept it small. Fifty dollars here. Fifty dollars there. Tiny amounts to someone with as much money as Rich. Amounts that could have been for any number of little things around the house. Going big would get him noticed, but skimming a little bit here and there he could keep this up forever, while still drawing a paycheque from the old lady to boot.

Kate Rich lived up to her name, with enough money in the bank to keep her well into her dotage without any trouble. She wouldn't have given any of those little cheques a second thought, and Henry's plan to defraud her would have gone perfectly if it weren't for the Smarts living up to their name, too. They had always suspected that something was awry with Henry and Ottis, even if they'd never quite been able to put their finger on it. They had kept a close eye on them while they were under the Smarts' own roof, and they had half expected them never to show up in Texas. They were half right. Ottis had vanished. Henry was a changed man without him, and suddenly that little girl Becky who they thought might have been his daughter was his wife? It was all too strange, so they took a close look at the situation, trying to find anything out of place.

In her finances, they found about a hundred and fifty dollars out of place, taken in small amounts over time. When Kate asked Henry to account for the missing money and set her fretting daughter's mind at ease, he responded by vanishing. Neither he nor Becky came back to work the next day, and nobody had any means of contacting him. Kate was prepared to forgive and forget, but O'Bere took personal offence at the man she had sheltered for all those months. The man now trying to rob her mother. So she filed a police report that would later prove instrumental in bringing Lucas's campaign of terror to an end.

Back at the House of Prayer, Henry was ready to pack his bags and get out of town before both Becky and Ruben himself intervened. They took turns extolling the virtues of their current living situation to Henry. Ruben was happy to put them up rent-free until Henry got a new job. Becky had found herself surrounded for the first time by a community that wasn't judging her as inferior, where she didn't have to hide anything to be accepted. This 'new normal' was giving her the self-confidence to speak out even when she wasn't desperate, and she had no intention of throwing it away for nothing. Between the two of them, they managed to convince Henry to stay put, and by the next morning, he had a new job on one of the Reverend's roofing crews.

A month rolled by, then another, with no excitement to speak of. Becky and Henry continued their sexual relationship, although it brought him very little joy—after so long, the hunt and the violence had become integral to his pleasure. He wasn't like Ottis, needing to kill every time he wanted sexual satisfaction, but he needed more than the timid fumblings of some love-sick teenager. He missed his old life. He missed Ottis. But even the things that used to be reliable reminders of that old life were being eroded in the House of Prayer.

Becky was becoming a believer. She thought that she could seek salvation from her former life in prayer and virtue, that she could become more than the white trash that everyone had always assumed that she was. She might well have succeeded if for a single moment she had let go of her tight grip on the weighty anchor of Henry. When Henry looked at her now, he could barely see Ottis in her face. He could barely remember why he had ever wanted her. He did his best to ignore her new Jesus talk, did his duty in the bedroom, and brought home enough money for them to eat.

There was no liquor in the House of Prayer collective, and that wore on him heavily. Just as Becky was revelling in no longer having to hide anything, Henry was feeling like he was under the most intense scrutiny of his life. He couldn't go out drinking. He couldn't go out looking for girls to prey on. He was trapped. Pinned in place on this blank spot on the map by obligation to a girl he could barely stand to talk to anymore. Things would come to a head soon. His temper would boil over and he'd take off into the great wide nowhere all over again. Maybe he'd find Ottis, maybe he'd go it alone. But he never got the opportunity. Becky's personal growth and ever-growing belief in the teachings of the Reverend Ruben Moore had finally reached the point where she felt ready to confront her old demons. She was old enough now that the system in Florida was unlikely to try to seize control of her again. And if it did, well then that was surely a small penance to pay in return for the forgiveness of her family. She came to Henry with a simple request. She wanted him to take her back to Florida. Away from all of this. He could not have been happier to oblige.

When they set off in the car, it brought a flood of good memories back to Henry. It reminded him of just how sweet their life had been and gave him hope that the two of them could get back to that. There were a lot of states between Texas and Florida. A whole lot of fun was waiting just beyond the horizon. The kind of fun that he'd been missing out on while he was shackled to a job and a home and a wife. Henry wanted to turn back the clock and start over with Becky, to get things back to the way they used to be when he was so happy just to see her. Sadly, the person who she used to be no longer existed.

It didn't take long into their journey before Becky started laying out the reasoning behind her pilgrimage home. She had done wrong in her life, she had sinned in more ways that she could readily count, and she knew in her heart that she would not be forgiven and granted a place in Heaven if she did not try to make apologies and amends to those she had left in her wake. Henry just nodded along to all the Jesus stuff the way that he always had. Soon she'd start badgering him to get on board with it, too, and he'd change the subject enough times that she'd eventually give up. 'Confession is the first step to forgiveness, you know?'

That pulled him out of his reverie. Confession was a very dangerous word. If Becky wanted to confess to all of her sins, she would most assuredly be tarring him with the same brush, and while she had seen some portion of the evil he'd done, she had no idea just how dark the path he'd tread had gotten. If she was out there running her mouth about all the bad things they'd done together, it was just a matter of time before it came back on him and people started looking into his history more closely than he would like. 'But ain't you just going to upset folk all over again? Rehashing all the bad stuff you did to them? Ain't it better to let it lie?'

It was the first time Henry had spoken since Becky had broached the subject, and even if he was arguing with her, at least he was talking. If he would talk and listen, then maybe all of this was fixable.

'It ain't about what is easy for them or for me, it is about what is right. There's wounds that can't never heal if you just keep covering them over. Reverend Ruben says you got to shine a light on the dark places. Uncover them secrets that are hurting y'all.'

Henry bit back his first reply. 'But some secrets is there to protect folk. You go telling everyone everything then their feelings are going to get hurt, or worse.'

'Reverend Ruben says...'

'I've heard about enough of what Ruben says. Now listen to what I say. You go running around making sad eyes and sorries to all your folks, and it is just going to bring a whole heap of trouble down on us. You want to go to jail? You thought juvie was bad, you ain't seen nothing until you get to a state prison. Think that you and me'll have a life together then?'

She turned her eyes back to the dark highway. Steeling herself. 'You got to make sacrifices to do the right thing. Sometimes that's how it is. 'Specially if you've done wrong.'

'So you just don't care that I'll be gone?' Henry's voice came out in a harsh whisper. 'You don't want me no more?'

She didn't have an answer for that. Henry was no longer the centre of her universe. She was still profoundly attached to him, but as she got older, the cracks in his façade were starting to show, and she was starting to think about her life as her own instead of as some part in a white trash fairytale romance. By the time she was old enough to drink, he'd be fifty. By the time she was his age, he'd likely be dead and gone. Even before she started to seriously consider the immorality of his life, she had that age difference to contend with, and while the attention of an older man had been flattering as a child, now she felt like she could see Henry clearly. They rode on in silence for a time, then almost without warning, Henry pulled off the road into a truck stop just outside of Bowie, Texas.

Inside the cafe, Henry made good use of the free coffee and facilities, and when the waitress came around they had as good a meal as a truck stop could provide. All of this was conducted in frosty silence. Henry didn't have a thing to say to Becky right then. His mind had turned back to the old subject of survival, and the least painful way to maintain his freedom.

They walked around the back of a trailer, heading for their car, and the neon of the truck stop blinked out, leaving them in nothing but moonlight. Becky turned to him, skin glowing in the darkness, and he could see that same old smile on her face, the one that said she was a little nervous but she trusted him to see her through. He closed his eyes as his fingers tightened around her throat. At least this was the end of it.

When he opened his eyes again, Becky was gone. The girl that he had fallen for all those years ago had emptied out of this body like water spilled from a glass. Now there was just another girl, another set of motions to go through to maintain his freedom. It was easier now that she wasn't watching. By the time he'd made it out into the middle of nowhere, he couldn't even recognise that the body used to be Becky. He drew out his machete and set to work, severing each of the limbs at the joints, taking off the head and burying it by the roadside before heading out into the big dark emptiness to scatter the other parts to the wind. It wasn't Becky. Not anymore.

Afterwards, Henry just sat in the car and tried to plan his next move. Even that simple a process was hard when he was feeling so numb, so he had to trust his instinct. He couldn't lie to Ottis. He couldn't go back to Florida and face the uncle of the girl he'd just butchered with any hope of seeing love on that man's face ever again. It was too soon, too raw. He needed some time to get that final image of her face out of his mind. He needed to move. He needed to run as far away as he could get. But to do that, he was going to need some money. Luckily enough, he knew somebody who had cash to spare.

The Downward Spiral

Kate Rich hadn't forgotten about Henry and Becky, despite the long months since the last time she had seen them. She had asked about town for them on occasion, even though she often struggled to get out and about on her own. She had felt some kinship with Becky when the girl was still around—seen some hint of her younger self in those big, sad eyes. Kate didn't know every detail of her situation, but she suspected plenty based on the interactions she'd witnessed between Henry and the girl. So when somebody came hammering at her door in the late evening, she half expected to walk down the stairs and find a runaway teenage girl waiting for her. Henry was an unwelcome surprise. 'What exactly do you want, Mister Lucas? Haven't you had enough from me already?'

His eyes were red like he'd been crying. 'I'm sorry, Mrs Rich, but I didn't know who else to turn to. You were always a good friend to us, and I feel just terrible about how things happened. It's Becky, you see. She's gone missing and we don't have any other people in these parts that I can ask for help. We're all alone out here.'

That stopped her dead in her tracks. 'Becky is missing, you say? You'd better come in then.'

Henry slunk in, eyes darting up and down the street like he was visiting his mistress. What a strange man. Kate shook the thought away, this was hardly the time. 'Now why don't you tell me exactly what happened, so I can help you.'

'We got in a fight, she was mad at me and she stormed off. We was at a truck stop, heading back south to see her folks, and she just ran off and now I don't know what to do to find her. Won't you help me?'

'Well, I'd say it sounds like she doesn't want you to find her.' Kate pursed her lips. 'Or that you're spinning me a yarn.'

Henry's sorrowful expression melted away into a grin. 'What is it about old bags like you that they can always see right through you?'

'Once burned, twice shy. That is what they say.' She straightened up to meet his smirk. 'So you're here with some deception to rob me once again? You must realise that I shall tell the police everything.'

Henry stepped closer. 'I don't reckon you'll be telling anyone much of anything by the time I'm through with you.'

Henry didn't often kill older women. His preference had always been for the young and the pretty when he had the choice, but he made do with the materials that were available to him. He strangled Kate Rich with his bare hands, feeling her papery skin tear beneath his digging fingers. Then he raped her, just the same as he had raped every other woman that he had killed, except the last. After he was finished, he took her out into one of the outbuildings and carved her into pieces, the same way that he had taught Ottis to do. And just like he had shown Ottis, he spent the rest of that night burning each and every one of those pieces until no trace remained, in an old wood-burning stove.

There was little cash in the house when all was said and done, far less than Henry had imagined that rich people kept lying around. And with no means of extracting a signature from the pile of ashes in the outhouses, the chequebook could serve him no purpose either. He set the house back to normal, cleaned away any trace that he had been there, and left quietly in the early hours of the morning, with just enough money to keep his car fuelled as he made his mad dash for freedom.

The luck that had preserved Henry through all of his life was finally starting to run thin. The world had changed while he wasn't looking, and the lifestyle that he was accustomed to had become a thing of the past. Nobody wanted itinerant workers anymore. Technology was booming, cities were growing and everywhere that civilisation blossomed was anathema to a man like Henry, who survived solely by slipping through the cracks. He took on a couple of temporary jobs across the southern states but soon found that he couldn't hold on to them when a simple background check threw all of the details of his officially recognised criminal past up as a barricade. With all of his dreams dead and buried behind him, he turned to the west and rode off for California once more.

The money ran out fast. Henry was drinking a lot to keep his feelings down, and keeping himself in a hazy state of not thinking cost more than keeping the car rolling. Without any work to support him, he thought that he might turn back to petty theft, the way that he had as a teenager, but like all of his other crimes, it seemed to have lost its appeal now. Perhaps, in time, his appetite for destruction and evil would have come back to him, but in the short-term, he still needed to get by.

His family no longer wanted anything to do with him. Stories of his child molestation had spread far and wide, and the cultural shifts of the late 70s and early 80s put far more condemnation on that than before. The things that he considered normal were now abhorrent. Even the squirrel raping half-brothers of his youth now looked down on him with disgust and contempt. All of Viola's children had gotten out of the Virginia woods; they had done their best to make something of themselves, something more than the feral children that their mothers made of them. All of them except Henry—the painful reminder of where they came from, and what they had been.

So, with no safety net left, and just a few stolen dollars left in his pockets, Henry decided to revisit a few old friends. The Smarts were absolutely gobsmacked when they answered the phone and found Henry on the other end. The moment that she realised who was on the line, O'Bere started screaming at him for robbing her mother. She was already on to the third round of expletives when Jack managed to wrestle the phone out of her hand. He clamped one of his hands over her mouth until she stopped flailing, then lifted the phone to his ear. As surprised as he had been to realise Henry had called, it was nothing compared to his surprise that Henry was still on the line after all of that screaming. 'Sorry about that, Henry. Big misunderstanding about that money situation. How are you doing?'

O'Bere was fuming, but it soon dawned on her what her husband was doing, so she kept her mouth shut as he nodded along and made sympathetic noises as Henry spun a tale of woe and abandonment, repeating the same lies over and over, like he was trying to wear through the truth by repetition alone. Eventually, when Henry felt like he was being believed, he asked if they still needed help with their furniture restoration business. He was alone now, and would only require a fraction of the room and board that his little family had required the last time around. He was down on his luck. It would be an act of charity. Jack wasn't enough of a fool to bring Henry to their doorstep. He quickly spun a sad story about their business going under but produced an alternative solution. He had a friend that lived just a little down the road, who was looking for help on his ranch. Would Henry be up for some odd jobs? It was just the bait that was required to reel the man in.

The next day, Henry completed the long drive to California and followed the instructions that he'd jotted dutifully down on a napkin until he arrived at the whitewashed gate of the ranch described. A police car pulled onto the dirt road behind him, flashing its blue and red lights in his rear-view mirror. Henry let out a groan. Jack Smart had set him up.

The Smarts and Henry never interacted the whole time he was in Hemet. They had made their statements to the police before Henry even arrived, and had now returned home to await whatever results the criminal justice system could dole out. News of Kate's absence had reached them only a few days before Henry arrived, and they did not consider it to be a coincidence that an elderly woman who had been taken advantage of by the man once had now decided to leave town alone in the middle of the night without telling anyone. With some distance from their time together and the opportunity to shake off the charismatic spell he'd laid over them, they now believed that Henry was dangerous. They had presented all of their suspicions to the police, alongside the evidence that they had collected of Henry's petty fraud.

The detective who had investigated the case came to their home twenty-four hours later and sat with them for a while. Henry had been released. There just wasn't sufficient evidence to hold him, and they had no way of corroborating the story that the Smarts had laid out for them when the Texas police were treating the case as nothing more than a matter of some dementia-riddled old woman wandering off. Even the fraud charges lacked sufficient evidence to hold Henry. Despite all of their suspicions and his outright refusal to answer even a single question, there was no legal reason to hold him any longer.

Henry fled from civilisation along the backroads, convinced that he was still under police surveillance, uncomfortably sober for the first time in weeks. He needed somewhere to lay low until this heat died down. He had to find someplace where the police and civilisation didn't encroach. Somewhere that would be called 'off the grid' in modern parlance.

Never one to repeat the same mistake twice, Henry didn't call ahead to the House of Prayer before arriving. The Reverend Ruben Moore was shocked to see the man returning after he'd vanished in the night, but he was even more surprised that Becky wasn't with him. It immediately set alarm bells ringing in his mind. Ruben wasn't an idiot any more than Jack Smart was. He may have been more focused on trying to see the best in people, but he wasn't blind to their faults. You couldn't run a commune that offered housing to drug addicts and career criminals without having some awareness, or you wouldn't live very long. On top of that awareness, he had his finger on the proverbial pulse in the area surrounding his little slice of heaven, constantly taking stock of the opinions being voiced so that he might more easily shelter his little flock from any vengeful souls who blamed them for those who wronged them. He knew all about Henry's dealings with Kate Rich, and he had heard all of the rumours about the old woman's disappearance. She wasn't some drifter that Henry had found at the roadside. She was a pillar of the local community, and when she went missing, she was missed.

While he was loathed to bring the attention of the police to the House of Prayer, his suspicions about Henry did not stop there. He had watched Becky's blind devotion to Henry and the older man's contempt for it. He knew that she would never have parted from him willingly, and when he was pressed, Henry gave up the same story as he'd rolled out before about arguing with her at a truck stop and her taking off with some lorry driver without a backward glance, exactly the way that Henry once had.

Moore found a space for Henry to sleep, promised him shelter from the dangers of the world, and a guarantee of work when there was some. He did exactly what a preacher was meant to do and took all of the man's worries away. Then, the moment that Henry was asleep, Ruben drove into town to find the sheriff.

Ruben Moore had an excellent relationship with local law enforcement, out of necessity, and he really couldn't have the people in his care seeing him betray the trust of any one of them if he hoped to maintain control over them. Having Henry in custody was important to the local police, but not so important that they could overlook the hornet's nest of potential trouble that the House of Prayer could represent if its equilibrium were disrupted. It was agreed that they would keep an eye out for

Henry's car about town and perform a traffic stop. All that Ruben had to do now was send the man on an errand.

The next morning, on June 15, 1983, Henry rolled into town and was stopped by a Texas Ranger named Phil Ryan. A cursory inspection of the inside of his vehicle revealed an unregistered handgun. As a felon, it was illegal for Henry to possess such a weapon. They finally had the excuse that they needed to arrest him, and once they had him, there wasn't a chance in hell that he was going to be allowed to walk free until he answered for whatever he had done to Kate Rich.

Anything You Say

The standard operating procedure of the local police seemed to be slightly overlooked when it came to Henry Lee Lucas. He was read his rights during the arrest, but when he tried to invoke them later, he discovered that those invariable rights afforded to every American seemed to vanish in the face of the murder of an old woman. He was stripped down to his undergarments as part of a 'weapon search,' but his clothes were never returned to him. He was deposited in a freezing concrete cell in between bouts of questioning. The police were mysteriously unwilling to fetch him his cigarettes, and when he complained of hunger and thirst, they brushed right past that into more demands for answers. Requesting a lawyer just resulted in him being flung back into the cell to wait for another hour while they 'tried to find one for him'. This was repeated over and over for almost four days, with each new shift of cops coming in and trying their luck.

Everyone knew that Henry had something to do with the disappearance of Kate Rich—they had the previous report of him defrauding her to tie him to an otherwise impregnable case. He was their only lead, and they were going to make him confess, one way or the other. It was only when they changed their tactics as they headed into the second day that they began to get a response from Henry. They started asking after Becky. Henry almost immediately lost his mind, trying to fling himself bodily over the table to attack the grinning deputy. He had to be restrained and dragged back to his cell to cool off. They had found the lever that they were going to use to pry the case open.

It took a solid hour of questioning before he told them his well-practiced story about Becky running off at a truck stop, and officers were despatched immediately once the timeline of events had been established, to find evidence to the contrary. What they discovered instead was a waitress who remembered Henry and Becky arguing as they left, just as he described. She suspected that she'd seen the girl getting into one of the trucks and driving off, but she couldn't recall for certain. It completely supported Henry's version of events, so the police ignored it. With the very real possibility that it was a dead end, and with Henry having spent another few hours in the freezing cell, they switched back to questioning him about Kate Rich. All that they needed was some small admission of guilt from him and the floodgates would open. Any slight mistake and they could pounce on it. They had him talking now, even if it was just to deny everything, and from there they could tie him to places and dates. They could find the hole in the story and dig through it to the truth, or at least to a plausible enough confession that they could use. Henry still had the same calculating look in his eyes that he'd had from the moment he arrived. Despite everything that had happened, he was still trying to work out how he could turn the situation to his advantage, how he could survive and thrive when all of the rules had been changed.

He took a deep breath and confessed to everything they had accused him of, at least in regards to Rich. He claimed that he couldn't remember where he had burned the old woman's body, but he admitted to strangling her to death, just as he had. As if by magic, a lit cigarette appeared in his hand and his lost clothes were found. A hot meal was fetched in for him, made to order exactly the way he liked it. He went from being lower than the lowest worm to being every cop's favourite person. So, he just went on talking—clumsily providing details that would later be enough to guarantee his conviction—right up until the moment that they came back in with a fresh pack of cigarettes and a typed confession for him to sign. He signed it readily, with only a small handwritten addendum on the last page: 'I am not allowed to contact anyone. I'm in here by myself and still can't talk to a lawyer on this. I have no rights so what can I do to convince you about all this?'

Henry was already in jail by the time that he met his appointed defence lawyer. Ron Ponton took one look at the confession, talked to Henry for all of five minutes, then had it officially recanted. The confession had been extracted under so much duress it would be almost impossible for any court to give it credence. In their rush to convict Henry, they had actually rendered the only real evidence that they had useless. Of course, that wasn't the only front that Ponton had to fight this case on. The sheriff was not running a watertight operation. The police had allowed so much information about the case to leak— including almost every detail of Henry's confession—that any random attention seeker off the street could now walk in and duplicate it. They hadn't just made Henry's confession worthless, they made any confession made by any other suspect worthless, too. The police had been so confident that they had their killer that they had skipped ahead several steps and started to influence the potential jury pool in favour of their case.

Ponton fought fire with fire, unleashing an incendiary statement to the press that turned the whole police department against him for years to come. He described the inhumane treatment that Henry had suffered through, adding that it was 'calculated solely to require my defendant to confess guilt, whether he was innocent or guilty'. The open and shut case had just been blown wide open all over again, and the police were looking to their forensics teams to make up for their failings.

In the wood-burning oven at Kate Rich's house, a single blackened bone fragment was found and confirmed to be human, but because of the heat it had been exposed to, there was no way to extract any more information from it. It could have been Kate's or anyone else's. There was even a marginal chance that it wasn't even a human bone. Henry's countermeasures had done well. Beyond that bone, there were traces of Henry around the Rich house, but it was a matter of record that he had worked there for some time, so there was no way of knowing precisely when those samples originally arrived. Faced with a dead end in that regard, but still certain of Henry's guilt, even if the confession couldn't be used in court, they decided to apply pressure from another angle.

The search for Frieda 'Becky' Powell's body was arduous and slow. They had only the location of the truck stop in Bowie and a vague timeline of the events that took place, but from that, they were able to extrapolate a circle in which it was likely that her body had been dumped. From there they narrowed their search to areas that were more isolated and therefore more likely. Piece by piece, they found the girl's body, and the forensics team painstakingly reassembled it. When they had as much as they could find put together, they could confirm that it was the remains of a girl, likely in her late teens. But beyond that, identification was impossible. Without the missing head, dental records were useless. They couldn't even place the time of death with any accuracy. There was definitely a dead teenager near to where Henry last claimed to have seen Becky, but beyond that, they could be certain of nothing.

Still, the few pieces of circumstantial evidence that they had managed to accrue, accompanied by Henry's now discredited confession, were likely to prove enough to see him convicted of both murders. The specific details that he had let slip about the murder of Rich were too specific to have come from somebody who was not involved, and he was the only one with any motive whatsoever to do harm to young Frieda Powell. It would be enough to convince a jury, and that was all that the prosecutors cared about.

When Henry had his day in court, he pleaded guilty to both of the murders with something resembling pride, rather than allow Ponton to do his job and fight the case that the state had built. None of this was particularly unusual, but what happened next was much more interesting—at the end of his confession in open court to killing both Frieda Powell and Kate Rich he added, 'And I've killed about a hundred other women, too.' His lawyer nearly lost his mind, but Henry hissed to him. 'If they're going to make me confess to one I didn't do, then I'll confess to everything.'

It was a kind of legal suicide. Henry didn't care about ever being free again. He barely even cared about staying alive. Everything that he had cared about was gone, and he had killed it with his own two hands. He received two life sentences for his crime, which he did nothing to dispute or appeal. Then, he was taken off to Williamson County Jail, where he was meant to live out the remainder of his days. In any sane world, that was where Henry's story would have come to an abrupt end, but his wild claims had already caught the attention of the serial killer obsessed media and the Attorney General of Texas. His confession might have been a bald-faced lie, but it was one that both of those powerful forces could use to their advantage, so they seized on it.

The only person who could have contradicted Henry and put an end to the impending circus was his fellow killer, Ottis Toole. But Ottis had his own problems to contend with at that moment in time. On his arrival back in Jacksonville after leaving Henry and Becky, Ottis had found the police already waiting on the doorstep of his sister's house. He went into custody expecting some follow-up questions about his missing niece, so it is safe to say that he was surprised when the police presented him with not one but two murder by arson charges. Henry's training had protected Ottis from forensics in all of the direct murders that they had conducted since meeting, but when it came to his old hobby of setting buildings alight, his technique hadn't improved since he was fourteen years old. Eyewitnesses put him at the scene of each crime, but the physical evidence required to pin both fires to him was just out of reach for the forensics of the time. His car was impounded for inspection and he was cut loose, with a warning that if he tried to leave town he would be jailed—evidence or not.

For the following year, he lived in a state of limbo, barely scraping by on the sufferance of his family and the few odd dollars he managed to make stripping wrecked cars, just like Henry had taught him. His true passions for murder and mayhem seemed to wither with nobody to share them with, and when science had advanced enough to tie him with certainty to the killings that he was suspected of, he went quietly, with a reserved sadness that nobody might have guessed that the loud and lumbering monster of a man was capable of.

Without Henry, he had no reason to live free, and he had no reason to fight against the charges that were levelled against him. He readily confessed to both of the arson charges and the accompanying murders in a plea deal that kept him out of reach of the electric chair. He was to serve two consecutive life sentences for his crimes, just like Henry. And, just like Henry, he was about to discover the incredible power of telling a lie that everybody wants to believe.

By December of 1983, Henry's story had filtered through to Ottis, even in prison, and he followed his lover's lead gleefully, stopping a passing guard with a flirtatious wink. 'Oh, officer, I've done some real bad things, and I want to talk about them.'

Before Henry had even been deposited in Williamson County Jail, where he was meant to spend the rest of his days, the Texas Rangers had already descended upon him. They formed the 'Lucas Task Force,' taking his confessions of serial murder completely at face value and using him to clear two hundred and thirteen previously unsolved murders through his confessions.

For the first time in his life, Henry was being treated well by other people. More than well, in fact. He was a celebrity, getting preferential treatment everywhere he went. He travelled the country on a private jet, staying in fancy hotels, eating in restaurants and cafés everywhere that he stopped, and generally being treated like royalty. In the police stations where he spent most of his time during each phase of confessions, he was given free rein to wander about, even being granted security codes to open the doors. He wore his own clothes, rarely had to wear handcuffs, and was treated more like a consultant than a convict.

In Huntington, West Virginia, Henry confessed to killing a man whose death had been ruled a suicide. That confession was sufficient to force the insurance company to pay out on his 'victim's' life insurance policy, granting a widow the financial aid that she needed to survive without her husband. The Rangers were delighted—they spent $3,000 dollars throwing Lucas a party in the Holiday Inn, bringing in liquor and prostitutes to celebrate their 'big win.'

Henry's confessions were absolutely perfect, with video and audio recordings of each one, and specific details being offered up that nobody except the investigators and the killer would know. The only problem was, some of them directly contradicted the others. Henry was possessed of a certain animal cunning, and he was a talented manipulator, but he was not an intelligent man by any stretch of the imagination. The dates of several of the murders that he confessed to did coincide, but they would have required some remarkable acts of transportation to make them possible, including a memorable five-thousand-mile cross-country drive in twenty-four hours.

Normal arrangements had been suspended around Henry Lee Lucas, and the end result was that he was gaining access to information about the crimes that he would later confess to ahead of time. He had computer access in some of the police departments that he visited. He was shown pictures of crime scenes ahead of time to 'jog his memory.' He even read through the police's reports while they set up their recording equipment just to 'make sure he got it all straight.'

This was the most comfortable that Henry had ever been, and he was making sure to milk it for all that it was worth. His prison cell in Williamson County was fitted out with all of the modern conveniences, including a television, a proper bed, and a small wardrobe for his clothes, as he was not obliged to wear a prison uniform. When he was on the road, he would often issue orders to the Texas Rangers who were supposed to be guarding him, and local police would marvel as they scampered off to fulfil his every whim. As long as his confessions kept on flowing, he was going to be living the high life, and he conveyed as much through his letters to Ottis, who quickly adopted the same 'tell them what they want to hear' attitude, supporting Henry's narratives where it suited him and contradicting them when he felt like it.

The duo were in frequent telephone contact despite all of the ways that this could taint the evidence that they provided, and at some point they decided that they wanted to create some bigger story out of their crimes and their lies; some grand, American drama played out through the medium of their confessions that would absolve both of them of guilt while still allowing them to reap the harvest of rewards that their confessions brought along with them.

Ottis's childhood provided them with exactly the inspiration that they needed—and so the Hands of Death were born.

Fruit of the Poisoned Tree

Every new confession that Henry gave now came with an introduction, relating to the orders he was issued by the shadowy and mysterious cult known only as the Hands of Death. He claimed that he, Ottis, and many of the other serial killers active in the USA throughout the 70s and 80s were not independent psychopaths as had been previously assumed, but were, in fact, all servants of a Satanic organisation that was using the mayhem that they spread to destabilise America.

It seems like an absolutely ridiculous supposition to the modern reader, but at the time, the 'Satanic Panic' was in full swing. A significant portion of the American people believed that there were devil worshipping cults hiding in plain sight all over the country and that the declining fortunes of America after the boom years following the Second World War could be blamed on infernal influence. As the years of 'flower power' and the hippie counterculture came to an end, all of the abuses of power within the communes and cults of that time period became public knowledge. Combined with some high-profile cases where Satanism was blamed for crimes involving child abuse, this created a surprisingly credulous audience for Henry's stories.

It isn't clear if Ottis ever crossed paths with any Satanists beyond his grandmother, although he would gladly regale you with stories of black masses and cannibal feasts if he was given the opportunity. But the small amount of knowledge he had on the subject still vastly outstretched that of those investigating his claims. As with the false confessions, he and Henry were able to provide just enough real details to make their stories of satanic murder cults seem plausible.

The Florida police were sent out to trawl the Everglades, to search for the Hands of Death cult's secret headquarters, and all the while, Henry and Ottis were still spilling out more salacious details about their crimes in its service. About the girl that they abducted from the roadside and delivered to the Everglades to serve as a meal at the initiation of new members. About the other serial killers that they met who also worked for the advancement of the cult's great objective of destroying America.

With all of the yarns that they were spinning, it was hardly surprising that some of them became a little tangled, and it was even less surprising that eventually one of them was woven into a noose. The 'Orange Socks' case had captured national attention for a short while. It had the whiff of celebrity about it, and now that they had a full confession to the murder, the Texas State Attorney was more than ready to press charges. After consulting the police files, Henry had produced an almost perfect confession to the crime, and there was no evidence that immediately contradicted the idea that it may really have been him, so they pressed ahead with the case. Henry went quite happily into the courtroom, treating it as just another of the many days out that his pseudo-celebrity status in the prison granted him. The jury was shown the video of his confession, which had been heavily edited to remove the coaching and leading questions from the officers in the room at the time of recording. Henry made no attempt to argue with the video, although his lawyer—who had a slightly better grasp on the magnitude of the situation—was quick to contest the veracity of the confession on the basis of that editing, and on the basis that he was able to produce a recorded confession from a completely different murderer that would remove all blame, or at least greatly reduce his client's culpability for his crimes. For the first time, the contradictions that Henry and Ottis had introduced into their shared stories became an advantage—both men claimed to have killed 'Orange Socks,' but only one of them could have committed the act itself.

The jury preferred the evidence on television to the man in a suit who kept talking at them. Henry was convicted of the murder, which he took in his stride. He was coming up on fifty years old. An extended sentence meant nothing to him anymore, which was why he was so gleeful in confessing to every crime under the sun. He was smiling in the courtroom right up until the moment that the judge passed his death sentence. Suddenly, his smile fell away and he started talking in harsh whispers to his lawyer. He was not aware that death was on the table when he started all of this. After he had first been arrested, he was at the lowest point in his life, but now he was living like a king and he didn't want that to stop any time soon. He begged his lawyer to get him out of it, to fix things. So, an appeal was soon set in motion.

Even though he had suffered through that scare, it did nothing to slow Henry's roll when it came to confessions. The Lucas Task Force picked him up again just a few days later to go out and look at some more crime scenes. Unfortunately for Henry and Ottis, by this point, their claims were finally starting to garner some scrutiny. Several officers that the Lucas Task Force had interacted with had noticed the bizarre way that he was being treated, and the completely inappropriate way that he was being given access to case information ahead of his confessions. Enough complaints were filed that the Texas Rangers began to suffer some scrutiny, and as a result, they had to begin running a tighter ship, with a marked reduction in the information that they were feeding to Henry ahead of time. Of course, by this point, Henry was pretty much an expert at manufacturing convincing confessions and in avoiding any potentially contradictory details in his recitals. The lack of solid facts to build on made his confessions a little bit shakier, but no less elaborate.

After Henry confessed to thirteen separate and unrelated murders in Houston, he came to the attention of Dallas detective Linda Erwin. Erwin thought that Henry was a liar from the moment she read the first reports about him, but that last cluster were enough to push her over the edge into taking action. She contacted the Lucas Task Force about a murder that she had on the books, a cold case that sounded like a perfect fit for Lucas's victim profile. She wondered if they might be able to bring Lucas and take a look at it before they left town. Henry looked over the collection of pictures that she had brought from the case, eavesdropped on the conversations that she had with the Texas Rangers outside, and then delivered a confession riddled with enough details to easily convict him of the crime. It would all have been a normal day in the work of the Lucas Task Force if it weren't for the fact that Erwin had fabricated the entire case using old crime scene photos and a little bit of imagination.

She reported this to Phil Ryan in the Texas Rangers, and before long he was repeating the experiment regularly with the Lucas Task Force, feeding them the details of an invented case and watching as they extracted a confession that perfectly matched the case details. By this point, Henry had produced over three thousand separate confessions to crimes so widespread that it was nearing the point of ridiculousness. His devotion to the 'Hands of Death' story just made his claims even more incredulous. But even the idea that he had murdered three thousand people was nothing compared to some of the stories that he made up on the fly. He claimed to have been involved in the assassination of Jimmy Hoffa, through the cult's mob ties. He claimed to have starred in a series of snuff films, filmed in the cult's headquarters in the depths of the Everglades. He even claimed that when Jim Jones decided that the time had come to kill his followers in Jonestown, Henry and Ottis were the ones who had been called on to deliver the poison. If he had confessed to ambushing Neil Armstrong when he first stepped out onto the surface of the moon, it wouldn't have been any more insane than some of the stories that he was already trying to get people to accept. He was rewarded every time that he invented a ridiculous story, so he went on telling ridiculous stories. To the limited intellect of Henry Lee Lucas, no one confession was any more ridiculous than any other. Truth and lie had blended in his mind to the point that he genuinely could not distinguish between them.

No evidence could ever be found of the Hands of Death, despite a frankly ridiculous amount of effort being expended trying to track the satanic cult down and Henry's endless insistence that they definitely existed.

In the midst of all this nonsense, Henry began to recant confessions as and when it suited him, then later confess yet again to the same crimes with altered details. Whether he was trying to make his confessions seem more believable or simply to tangle the web even further for those trying to create actual prosecutions from his claims is unclear, but the end result was that almost nothing that he said was usable in a court of law, if only because his complicated system of confession, recanting, re-confession, and later denial of key details would make things too difficult for a jury to follow.

By 1986, almost every law enforcement agency in the country had learned that Henry's lies could not be trusted, and the jet-setting lifestyle that he was accustomed to had settled into a more comfortable and settled life on death row. The Attorney General for Texas, Jim Mattox, had seen his underlings using Lucas to clear the books of unsolved crimes and was disgusted with their betrayal of the system that they were sworn to uphold. He pushed through a report on the confessions and convictions connected to Henry Lee Lucas, informally known as 'The Lucas

Report,' which proved beyond a shadow of a doubt that most, if not all, of his confessions, were provably false.

Working through every single official record from Henry's life, they were able to construct a timeline of his movements throughout the years. There were huge grey areas when he worked cash in hand or drifted throughout the country, but specific confessions were soon easily discounted.

The murder of Curby Reeves in Smith County, Texas, occurred on August 10, 1977. Despite confessing to the crime and providing details that 'only the killer could know,' Henry was working a twelve-hour shift in a mushroom farm in Pennsylvania on that date. Similarly, the 1979 murder of Elaine Tollett in Tulsa, Oklahoma, occurred while Henry was hospitalised in Bluefield, West Virginia. Most pressingly, the murder of 'Orange Socks' in Texas coincided with a roofing job that Henry was recorded to have attended in Florida. It was possible that Henry altered those business records as a forensic counter-measure, or simply to claim wages that he was not entitled to, but the homeowner remembered him specifically. Henry remained adamant about his guilt, but the State of Texas was not prepared to kill a man when the only evidence that he had committed a crime at all was the word of a known liar.

Down in Raiford Prison in Florida, no attempts had been made to construct prosecutions out of Ottis Toole's confessions. Too much of his story was fluid. Too many of his confessions were circumstantially correct at best. Ottis was successfully convicted of a pair of additional murders over the years, but it was never as a result of his confessions, only solid police work, eyewitness testimony, and fresh evidence being uncovered. Two hitchhikers, David Schallart and Ada Johnson, were among his confessions, but DNA evidence on both bodies was what cinched both cases.

More years were added to his sentence, but the death penalty was never sought, not when it was clear that the years of appeals would all prove pointless in the face of Ottis's impending mortality anyway. Instead of making Ottis the centre of attention, the state of Florida let him wither away in darkness, and it took barely any time at all for his steady stream of confessions to run dry with no material reward. He lived a relatively comfortable life in the prison compared to the conditions that many of the other prisoners faced, but he wasn't elevated to a state of royalty like Henry, or Ted Bundy—who slept in the room beside his. The only real pleasure that Ottis seemed to find in his prison life was his weekly telephone call with Henry, where he was often overheard to express his undying love for the other man, even though he knew Henry couldn't return it. Even on their very last phone call, in 1996, when a phone had to be brought to the side of his bed in the medical wing, Henry never told Ottis that he loved him. A lifetime of alcoholism and hard living caught up to Ottis on September 15, 1996, when, at the age of 49, his liver failed. His niece was the only one at his bedside to hear his final words—a deathbed confession that he was the one responsible for the death and decapitation of Adam Walsh, along with the sad story that accompanied it. Nobody came to claim Ottis's body, so he was buried in an unmarked grave in the prison cemetery. If Henry mourned his closest friend's death, he was careful to give no sign of it. Whatever his complicated feelings towards Ottis were, he kept them locked inside, never to be heard by any living soul.

As a result of the Lucas Report findings, in 1998, Governor George W. Bush commuted Henry's death sentence to life in prison—the only time that the future president would ever commute a death penalty in his whole career.

The Williamson County prosecutor, who had devoted no small part of his efforts through the years in trying to secure a conviction for the 'Orange Socks' case, felt simultaneously vindicated and furious about the whole thing. There had been other, far more viable suspects in the case that had now slipped beyond the reach of justice due to Henry's confessions, and there were likely to be thousands of other criminals still walking the streets because of his interference. For every actual serial killer who was annoyed that Henry had taken credit for their work, there were probably a hundred run-of-the-mill murderers delighted to have attention diverted away from them. Convictions based solely on confessions soon became a rarity in the American criminal justice system because of the actions of Henry Lee Lucas and Ottis Toole.

On March 13, 2001, Henry had been almost entirely forgotten. Even the criminologists and students who used to visit him had stopped after the findings of the Lucas Report proved that any statement he made was worthless. There had been a few crusaders over the years, people with a political interest in seeing Henry as being everything that he said he was, but they were out on the fringe, with no real power to change his life, so he ignored them. He remained in a state of relative comfort within the prison, never having to work for the privileges that other prisoners slaved away for thanks to the deals that he had cut during his rash of confessions. He was tucked up in a real bed, with a real mattress, in a state of comfort that those around him would never experience again, right up until the moment that his heart stopped beating.

The Perfect Liars

If you believed every part of Henry and Ottis's tales without doubt, then the duo were the most prolific and dangerous serial killers in American history. An urban legend come to life: one of them a towering, simpering monster who could only achieve orgasm through killing, the other a one-eyed drifter who exuded a literal miasma of evil.

The truth is a little more complex. Some of the events in this book may not have happened precisely as described. Not just the small details of the specific words that people used, the exact time of day, or the complexities of their motivations, but the actual crimes that formed the centre of Henry and Ottis's stories may not have happened at all. It is almost impossible to separate fact from fiction when it comes to these killers, and it is only by constant comparison between their stories, official records, eyewitness accounts, and every other available source that it is possible to piece together something that seems likely to be the truth.

Both men were devoid of empathy, interested in their own hedonistic pleasure above all else, and devoted to murder as the tool by which they could achieve their goals. They were psychopaths in the purest sense, shaped by biology and circumstance to pursue only their own interests to the exclusion of all else—and then they encountered the system that was meant to keep men like that away from civilisation. The prisons reshaped these crude killing animals into the perfect criminals, giving them the education that they needed to avoid detection for decades and providing them with plain evidence that their lives mattered more than the lives of their victims. Every act of evil that they ever committed was rewarded, both in the pleasure that it brought them and in the comfort that they would later enjoy in prison.

Despite the ridiculousness of their claim that there was some shadowy secret society providing Henry and Ottis with victims and a purpose in life, it turned out to be true. The criminal justice system that was supposed to stop men like them instead empowered them and rewarded them for their crimes.

Both of these men are, undeniably, serial killers—enough evidence has accrued over the years that this one seed of truth beneath the tangled mess of lies cannot be disputed. But beyond that, it all comes down to belief. Either they killed the forty people that criminologists have been able to tie to them with some degree of certainty, or they killed upwards of three thousand people while easily evading detection or capture for decades.

Ultimately, Henry and Ottis's greatest legacy is not their actions, but their stories. Clumsily constructed and blithely told, their tales made legends out of them in their own lifetime. The stuff of nightmares, certainly, but not the kind of nightmares that will readily be forgotten when dawn breaks. The kind that go on preying at your mind and come back to you every time you are lying down to sleep to fill you with dread. They did not kill all of the people that they said they did, but they could have. Anybody could be just as prolific and avoid detection just as easily. And that possibility is more frightening than any cold, hard facts.

TRUST ME

Want More?

Did you enjoy *Trust Me* and want some more True Crime?

YOUR FREE BOOK IS WAITING

From bestselling author Ryan Green

There is a man who is officially classed as "**Britain's most dangerous prisoner**"

The man's name is Robert Maudsley, and his crimes earned him the nickname "**Hannibal the Cannibal**"

This free book is an exploration of his story...

"Ryan brings the horrifying details to life. I can't wait to read more by this author!"

Get a free copy of **Robert Maudsley: Hannibal the Cannibal** when you sign up to join my Reader's Group.

www.ryangreenbooks.com/free-book

Every Review Helps

If you enjoyed the book and have a moment to spare, I would really appreciate a short review on Amazon. Your help in spreading the word is gratefully received and reviews make a huge difference to helping new readers find me. Without reviewers, us self-published authors would have a hard time!

Type in your link below to be taken straight to my book review page.

US   geni.us/trustmeUS

UK   geni.us/trustmeUK

Australia geni.us/trustmeAUS

Canada   geni.us/trustmeCA

Thank you! I can't wait to read your thoughts.

About Ryan Green

Ryan Green is a true crime author who lives in Herefordshire, England with his wife, three children, and two dogs. Outside of writing and spending time with his family, Ryan enjoys walking, reading and windsurfing.

Ryan is fascinated with History, Psychology and True Crime. In 2015, he finally started researching and writing his own work and at the end of the year, he released his first book on Britain's most notorious serial killer, Harold Shipman.

He has since written several books on lesser-known subjects, and taken the unique approach of writing from the killer's perspective. He narrates some of the most chilling scenes you'll encounter in the True Crime genre.

You can sign up to Ryan's newsletter to receive a free book, updates, and the latest releases at:

WWW.RYANGREENBOOKS.COM

More Books by Ryan Green

In July 1965, teenagers Sylvia and Jenny Likens were left in the temporary care of Gertrude Baniszewski, a middle-aged single mother and her seven children.

The Baniszewski household was overrun with children. There were few rules and ample freedom. Sadly, the environment created a dangerous hierarchy of social Darwinism where the strong preyed on the weak.

What transpired in the following three months was both riveting and chilling. The case shocked the entire nation and would later be described as "The single worst crime perpetuated against an individual in Indiana's history"

More Books by Ryan Green

MAN EATER

THE TERRIFYING TRUE STORY OF CANNIBAL KILLER KATHERINE KNIGHT

On 29th February 2000, John Price took out a restraining order against his girlfriend, Katherine Knight. Later that day, he told his co-workers that she had stabbed him and if he were ever to go missing, it was because Knight had killed him.

The next day, Price didn't show up for work.

A co-worker was sent to check on him. They found a bloody handprint by the front door and they immediately contacted the police. The local police force was not prepared for the chilling scene they were about to encounter.

Price's body was found in a chair, legs crossed, with a bottle of lemonade under his arm. He'd been decapitated and skinned. The "skin-suit" was hanging from a meat hook in the living room and his head was found in the kitchen, in a pot of vegetables that was still warm. There were two plates on the dining table, each had the name of one of Price's children on it.

She was attempting to serve his body parts to his children.

More Books by Ryan Green

In 1902, at the age of 11, Carl Panzram broke into a neighbour's home and stole some apples, a pie, and a revolver. As a frequent troublemaker, the court decided to make an example of him and placed him into the care of the Minnesota State Reform School. During his two-year detention, Carl was repeatedly beaten, tortured, humiliated and raped by the school staff.

At 15-years old, Carl enlisted in the army by lying about his age but his career was short-lived. He was dishonourably discharged for stealing army supplies and was sent to military prison. The brutal prison system sculpted Carl into the man that he would remain for the rest of his life. He hated the whole of mankind and wanted revenge.

When Carl left prison in 1910, he set out to rob, burn, rape and kill as many people as he could, for as long as he could. His campaign of terror could finally begin and nothing could stand in his way.

More Books by Ryan Green

CRIMSON PETTICOATS
THE BETRAYAL, BRUTALITY AND BLOODSHED BEHIND THE FRENCH MAID MASSACRES

In 1861, the police of a rural French village tore their way into the woodside home of Martin Dumollard. Inside, they found chaos. Paths had been carved through mounds of bloodstained clothing, reaching as high as the ceiling in some places.

The officers assumed that the mysterious maid-robber had killed one woman but failed in his other attempts. Yet, it was becoming sickeningly clear that there was a vast gulf between the crimes they were aware of and the ones that had truly been committed.

Would Dumollard's wife expose his dark secret or was she inextricably linked to the atrocities? Whatever the circumstances, everyone was desperate to discover whether the bloody garments belonged to some of the 648 missing women.

Free True Crime Audiobook

Sign up to Audible and use your free credit to download this collection of twelve books. If you cancel within 30 days, there's no charge!

WWW.RYANGREENBOOKS.COM/FREE-AUDIOBOOK

"Ryan Green has produced another excellent book and belongs at the top with true crime writers such as M. William Phelps, Gregg Olsen and Ann Rule" –**B.S. Reid**

"Wow! Chilling, shocking and totally riveting! I'm not going to sleep well after listening to this but the narration was fantastic. Crazy story but highly recommend for any true crime lover!" –**Mandy**

"Torture Mom by Ryan Green left me pretty speechless. The fact that it's a true story is just...wow" –**JStep**

"Graphic, upsetting, but superbly read and written" –**Ray C**

WWW.RYANGREENBOOKS.COM/FREE-AUDIOBOOK

Printed in France by Amazon
Brétigny-sur-Orge, FR